The
KINGDOM
of the
GODS

© The Theosophical
Publishing House, Adyar, 1952

First Edition 1952
First to Tenth Reprints 1953-1987
Eleventh Reprint 1997
Twelfth Reprint 1999

ISBN   81-7059-060-4 (Hard Cover)
ISBN   81-7059-292-5 (Soft Cover)

Printed at the Vasanta Press
The Theosophical Society
Adyar, Chennai 600 020, India

PLATE 10.

A MOUNTAIN GOD NATAL

DEDICATION

This book is gratefully dedicated to the late Ethelwynne M. Quail who in March, 1937, provided the illustrations based upon my researches, carried out between 1921 and 1929, during which period six books on the subject were published. Although widely projected as slides throughout the world, the pictures themselves were not published until this book first appeared in 1952.

GEOFFREY HODSON

ACKNOWLEDGEMENTS

Acknowledgements are gratefully made for financial help received from Theosophists in Java, New Zealand and America, from the Young Theosophists of Blavatsky Lodge of the Theosophical Society, Sydney, New South Wales, Australia, and Dr. W. M. Davidson of Chicago and his colleagues, who generously helped to meet the cost of publication.

I am especially grateful to my friends Roma and Brian Dunningham for their generosity throughout many years and the provision of much-needed stenographers.

" The philosopher should be a man willing to listen to every suggestion but determined to judge for himself. He should not be biased by appearances; have no favourite hypothesis; be of no school; and in doctrine have no master. Truth should be his primary object. If to these qualities he adds industry he may hope indeed to walk within the veil of the Temple of Nature."

FARADAY

PREFACE

THE successful study of the subject of the Angelic Hosts restores to its essential monotheism every apparently polytheistic religion. At the heart of every great World Faith is the concept of an Absolute, Unknowable, Infinite and Unchanging Source and Foundation. From this, at regular intervals, emanates the potentiality of divine Ideation as the purest abstraction. This is the reality behind the One God, however formalised, of all religions and especially of the esotericism of the Ancient Mysteries. At this stage in the process of emanation from the Absolute, unity alone exists. No later changes, no series of successive emanations from this ONE ALONE, alter the fact that the manifested Source is a Monad.[1]

By reflection of Itself in the eternal, pre-cosmic, virginal Space, the ONE is said thereupon to establish a dyad [2] which is positive-negative, male-female, potential father-mother in one Existence. It should be noted that not an actual but a reflected " Second Person " has now come into existence, or rather is conceived, after which numerical law assumes supreme rule of the process of emergence or emanation and objective appearance of creative Gods in multiplicity.

The positive and negative aspects of the ONE interact interiorly, as an androgyne, to produce an objective Third. This Third is not regarded as a self-separate unit, an independent existence. Monad, dyad, triad, remain as a

[1] *Monad*, Greek. The one invisible Self—the Unity; the eternal, immortal and indestructible human spirit. Vide *The Monad*, C. W. Leadbeater, T.P.H., Adyar.

[2] Sometimes incorrectly written duad.

trifunctioning unit, a three-in-one, behind and yet within the veil of pre-cosmic Substance.

An irresistible process has now been initiated. An omnipotent force has begun to emanate from Absolute Existence. The Three-in-one is propelled, as it were, towards objectivity and finiteness. The Triple God awakes and opens Its single eye. The triangle of light emits rays. These are inevitably seven in number. Sub-rays shine from them, each an intelligent Power, each a creative Logos,[1] each an Archangel of spiritual light.

Universal, divine Ideation becomes focused creative thought. The single, all-inclusive Idea passes through the phases of duality, triplicity and sevenfold expression into the almost infinite diversity potentially present in primordial thought. The purely spiritual has thus become manifest as the purely mental, which is formative and, by the ceaseless action of the propellent force, projects its Ideations as the Archetypes of Cosmoi, Solar Systems and all that they ever produce.

Numerical law, time in succession, involutionary and evolutionary processes, replace spaceless eternity. Divine thought sets up time-space conditions and in them produces material forms which increase in density until a limit has been reached. Thereafter, the whole process is reversed until limited time and space disappear into eternity, thus bringing the great cycle to a close.

The Angelic Hosts may be regarded as the active, creative Intelligences and form-builders of all objective creation. They are manifestations of the One, the Three, the Seven and all products thereof. From dawn to eve of Creative Day, they are ceaselessly in action as directors, rectors, designers,

---

[1] *Logos*, Greek. The manifested Deity who speaks the creative Word whereby universes spring into being and life. The outward expression of the Causeless Cause which is ever concealed. Adapted from Vol. 6, *The Secret Doctrine* and *The Theosophical Glossary*, H. P. Blavatsky.

artists, producers and builders, ever subservient to and expressive of the One Will, the One Substance and the One Thought.

In the exoteric aspects of ancient Faiths, these Beings, as also the underlying principles, the laws, the processes and the modes of manifestation of the creative force are personified, named and given traditional forms. Esoterically, however, these personifications were in no sense regarded as realities but rather as thought forms and symbols of major creative Powers and Beings. These symbols were partly invented by the Initiated Teachers of earlier peoples as aids to the masses for whom abstractions could possess no reality. Generations of worship gave to them durable concrete shapes in the mental world which served as links between the human mind and the realities which the symbols represented. These symbolic figures also served as channels through which the true Intelligences could be invoked and pour down Their beneficent influence, enlightening truths and occult forces for the helping of mankind.

These are the exoteric Gods of all religions, not to be confused with the Hosts of the Logos, the Archangels of the Face, the Sephiroth, the Angels of the Presence, the Mighty Spirits before the Throne, the physically invisible yet omnipresent manifestors and engineers of the one propellent Power by which alone all things are made and without which nothing was made that was made. From nature spirit to Cherubim, all these Intelligences make manifest—without the intervention of individuality—the One Divine Thought.

This is the foundation upon which this book is constructed. This is the idea underlying all its contents. This, I believe, is the key to a subject so vast and so important that complete comprehension and exposition of it are impossible to the purely human mind. Continued neglect of these teachings of the Arcane Wisdom by a race which is being led by science into knowledge and practical use of the one Creative Force—cosmic, solar and planetary electricity—of which Angelic Hosts are the chief and subordinate engineers, can lead to disastrous consequences, of which the Hiroshima and Nagasaki atom bombs might possibly be regarded as foreshadowings.

This work appears as man is thus learning to release physically, and under his control, atomic energy. Despite my great limitations of knowledge and power of exposition, it is my hope that, with other works on the subject of greater merit, this book may lead to the investigation and ultimate discovery of and reverence for the noumena behind phenomena and that One Presence and Power within which all things live and move and have their being.

The safeguards which can prevent man from self-destruction by the natural forces which he is now learning to employ are reverence, probity, morality. These qualities are amongst the greatest of the needs of modern man as he seeks world confidence, world security and the freedom from fear by which alone he can advance into an age rich with promise of lofty human achievement, material, cultural, intellectual and spiritual.

If, in addition, there is a single idea which emerges from a study of the Gods and an attempted presentation of the fruits of such study, that idea seems to me to be: "Man can know the facts. Faith need not be blind." Man is endowed with all the faculties necessary for complete knowledge both of himself and the visible and invisible universe. Extended vision is one of the required faculties. By its development and use, the boundaries of human knowledge may be gradually advanced until noumenon and phenomenon are fully investigated and ultimately known as one.

This fact is of importance, for at heart man is a seeker, an investigator, an explorer. Human life is a search, first for the ponderables that they may be possessed and give pleasure and security, and later that they may be shared. At last, shattered and frustrated by the impermanence of things tangible and visible, man turns towards the imponderables. Especially does he seek conviction founded upon immovable reality.

Guided by the methods and the findings of successful explorers, I have also begun to search. Whilst I think I have found out what the ultimate discovery is, its attainment is obviously, as yet, very far off. *En route*, certain experiences have been passed through, certain intermediate discoveries made. Since they seem to be interesting and useful in themselves and also have their place in reaching ultimate truth, I share them, hoping that they may inform and help others who similarly seek.

Knowledge when substantiated is valuable for its own sake. It is still more valuable if it can be applied to human welfare. The present approach of science to the idea that the universe is the product of creative thought and purpose renders valuable knowledge concerning the realm of universal mind in which, according to occult investigation, creative Intelligences are active.

Modern medicine proclaims the causes of many human illnesses to be in the mind and seeks to cure them by the correction of mental disabilities. Knowledge of the inhabitants of the plane of mind and of the agents which direct formative and corrective thought currents can, in consequence, be very helpful in healing the sick.

Information upon these subjects is offered in this book.

What then is the utlimate discovery, the Himalayan summit? At the heart of the Cosmos there is ONE. That ONE has Its sanctuary and shrine in the heart of every human being. The first major discovery is of this Presence within, " the Inner Ruler Immortal seated in the heart of all beings."

(*Bhagavad Gita.*)   Ultimately identity with the ONE ALONE, fully conscious absorption for evermore in the eternal, self-existent ALL, is attained. *This is the goal.*

As a mountaineering expedition includes geologists, botanists, surveyors and photographers who observe for the service of others the nature of the country, the foothills and the higher slopes leading to the summit, so the climber in the mountains of truth may usefully observe and describe the phenomena of the levels through which he passes. This book is a record of such observations.

Admittedly, knowledge concerning the Lesser and Greater Gods is not essential to the rediscovery of the inseparable unity and the identity of man-spirit and God-spirit which is the goal. Admittedly, also, unless used as a stepping stone from the unreal to the Real, for some temperaments, undue interest in external phenomena, physical or superphysical, can prove a distraction.

The controlled mind is, however, capable of directing its attention where it will and a controlled mind is essential to success in the Great Search. Few major attainments stand alone. Nearly all are led up to by preceding successes and discoveries which at the time were not necessarily regarded as leading to a greater truth. As long, therefore, as the ultimate goal is remembered, a study of the results of intermediate phases of illumination can assist, encourage, inspire and instruct.

The pure mystic, absorbed in contemplation of the Eternal One and in the ecstasy of union, is no longer interested in the external. Once the capacity for contemplation has been attained, naught else is needed. One-pointedly the exalted devotee pursues his path to the lotus feet of the Immortal One.

Men are not all mystics, though all must one day attain to the mystical union, each following his own road to bliss of which there are said to be seven. Upon one of them, especially, and possibly upon others, direct knowledge of the forces and Intelligences of Nature and acquirement of the faculty of co-operating with them in what is sometimes called the Great Work can be of much value. If, therefore, the contents of such a work as this seem to some minds to be irrelevant to the true purpose of the human life and the true nature of the human quest, I would draw attention to the words of a Great One: " However men approach Me, even so do I welcome them, for the path men take from every side is Mine." (*Bhagavad Gita*, iv, 11, translated by A. Besant.)

INTRODUCTION

ONE day [1] as, on a hillside at the edge of a beech forest in a secluded valley in the West of England, I was seeking ardently to enter the Sanctuary of Nature's hidden life, for me the heavens suddenly became filled with light. My consciousness was caught up into a realm radiant with that light which never was on land or sea. Gradually I realised the presence of a great Angelic Being, who was doubtless responsible for my elevated state. From his [2] mind to mine there began to flow a stream of ideas concerning the life, the force and the consciousness of the universe and their self-expression as angels and as men. This description is not strictly accurate, however, because during such communication, the sense of duality was reduced to a minimum. Rather did the two centres of consciousness, those of the angel and myself, become almost co-existent, temporarily forming one " being " *within* which the stream of ideas arose. This, I believe, is essentially true of all interchanges which occur above the level of the formal mind, and especially at those of spiritual Wisdom and spiritual Will. In the latter, duality virtually disappears and oneness, uttermost interior unity, alone remains.

Daily entering that realm of light, I found that the great ocean of the life, the force and the soul of the universe had its myriad denizens. These are the Spiritual Selves of men and Super-men and the vast company of the Angelic Hosts,

[1] In the year 1926.

[2] The masculine is used for convenience only, such Intelligences being asexual, though of dual polarity, the apparent preponderance of one or other " sex " varying in different Orders.

of which the Being who " addressed " me was a member. He was supernally beautiful, majestic, godlike, and impassive and impersonal to the last degree. As teacher to pupil, he began to tell of—and to enable me, with gradually increasing clarity, to perceive—the Angelic Hosts, their Orders and degrees. He told of their communion with men, as in ancient Greece, Egypt and Eastern lands, their place in Nature as Ministers of the Most High and of that great dawn of creation when, metaphorically, as the Morning Stars they sang together and as the Sons of God they shouted for joy. He spoke of the creative process as the composition and performance of a celestial symphony, of the Logos as Divine Musician and of His universe as a manifestation of celestial harmony. He told of the great Gods who assimilate the mighty creative chords in their primordial potency and relay them through all their ranks from the highest spiritual worlds to the realm of everlasting Archetypes, the great sound-forms upon and by which the physical universe is modelled. Therefrom, he said, the music of the Creative " Word " passes on to the lower worlds, where lesser Hosts formatively echo and re-echo it, thereby building all Nature's varied forms. Since the Great Artist of the Universe perpetually creates, the Creative Symphony is ever being composed and ever performed. Angels and men live amidst celestial harmonies, the everlasting music of the spheres.

Such, in part, is the vision which once I had and which still lives with me. With it there has come the knowledge that, in their real existence, the Gods who once were so near to men were none other than the Angelic Hosts, that throughout the great racial darkness they have still been near, though unperceived, and that the time approaches when again the Major Creative Powers and Beings, the laws by which Cosmos emerges from chaos and the place of humanity in the vast process of divine manifestation will become apparent to mankind. For that day, it was intimated, man may well prepare. Ugliness must be banished, war must be outlawed, brotherhood must reign, beauty must be enshrined in human hearts and revealed through human lives. Then to a humanity united in one fraternity the High Gods will reveal their immortal loveliness and lend their aid in building a new world in which all men may perceive and serve the Supreme as Beauty and as Truth.

GEOFFREY HODSON

Epsom,
Auckland, New Zealand,
1952.

CONTENTS

xxiii

PART I

FOUNDATIONS

CHAPTER I

DEFINITION OF TERMS

S INCE in this book certain familiar words are used in a special sense and certain ideas unfamiliar to most Western readers are presented, this first Chapter consists of a definition of terms and a brief exposition of the philosophic basis upon which the book is founded.

THE DEITY

In Occult philosophy, the Deific Power of the universe is not regarded as a personal God. Although imbued with intelligence, It is not *an* Intellect. Although using the One Life as vehicle, It is not Itself *a* Life. Deity is an inherent Principle in Nature, having Its extensions beyond the realm of manifested forms, however tenuous.

The Immanence of God is not personal, neither is the Transcendence. Each is an expression in time, space and motion of an impersonal Principle, which of Itself is eternal, omnipresent and at rest.

Finiteness is essential to the manifestation of THAT which is Infinite. Ideas, rhythms and forms are essential for the expression of THAT which is Absolute. God, then, may best be defined as Infinity and Absoluteness made manifest through finite forms. Such manifestation can never be singular or even dual alone; it must always be primarily threefold and secondarily sevenfold. Point, circumference and radii;

3

power, receiver and conveyer; knower, known and knowledge; these must ever constitute the basic triplicity without which Absoluteness can never produce finiteness, at however lofty a level.

Creation, therefore, involves a change from a unity to a triplicity. In order to become the many, the One must first become the three. The possible combinations of three are seven. Continuance of advance from unity to diversity inevitably involves passage through seven modes of the manifestation and expression of that which essentially is one. Thus divisions arise in the One Alone. Thus beings arise within the One Life and intelligences appear within Universal Mind, all inherent within the Whole.

Of the Trinity, the point is the highest because the Source. Of the Seven, the Trinity is the highest because the parent. Thus hierarchy exists when manifestation occurs Parent hierarchies give birth to offspring in a descending scale of nearness to the original Source. Emanated beings in hierarchical order inevitably come into existence when movement first occurs in THAT which of Itself is still.

Absolute stillness implies absolute motion, the two terms being synonymous. The Absolute, therefore, can be both still and in motion whilst retaining absoluteness. The finite is therefore contained within the Absolute, which in its turn enfolds and permeates the finite. Because of this, finite beings have regarded the Absolute as divine and have named it God.

The worship of the all-enfolding and all-permeating Source of all is true religion. To reverence the omnipresent Source and to conform to its laws of manifestation is true religious practice. To conceive the Source of all as a person, however exalted, and to give it human attributes, is not true religion. To reverence that false conception and live in fear of its vengeance is not true religious practice.

Absolute existence and absolute law—these are the highest existences and therefore are worthy of man's study and reverence. Finite existence and finite law are not the highest existences and therefore are not worthy of the title "God". They are offspring and not parent, secondary and not primary, and their elevation to primary rank can only lead to confusion and dismay.

Modern man needs to emancipate himself from the delusion and worship of a personal, and therefore finite, God, and to substitute therefore an impersonal and infinite Deific Power and Law, with Deific Life as the essential Third.

Deific Life is the vehicle of Deific Power, and Deific Law rules their combined expression. By the instrumentation of Life, therefore, all things truly were made. Life is the Creator Sustainer and Transformer of the Cosmos. Life should be reverenced in all its manifestations and such reverence of omnipresent, ever-active Life is true religion.

What, then, is Life to the human intellect? How may Deific Life be conceived, perceived and worshipped—that is the supreme problem. Life may be conceived as the soul of form, its relationship to which is comparable to that of the sun to the solar system. The difference between the two relationships is that Life is omnipresent and the sun has a fixed location, even though its rays pervade the universe. Life does not send forth rays; for as the interior source of existence, Life is all-pervading and all-penetrating.

Life is beneficent in that by it all things are sustained. Without it, nothing can exist that does exist. It is the Thought-Soul, the Spirit-Intelligence, of all Creation. Vehicle for Power imbued with ideative thought, Life is the one essential to existence, to evolution and to transfiguration. Life, then, is God and God is Life.

The term "God" thus implies all Nature, physical and superphysical, the evolutionary impulse imparted to it and the irresistible creative force which bestows the attribute of self-reproduction and the capacity to express it indefinitely. This concept of Deity includes the creative Intelligences—the Elohim—which direct the manifestations and the operations of the one creative force, the divine thought or Ideation of the whole Cosmos from its beginning to its end and the "sound" of the Creative "Voice" by which that Ideation is impressed upon the matter of Cosmos. All these, together with all seeds and all beings, forces and laws, including the one parent law of harmony, constitute that totality of existence to which in this work is given the title "God".

If so vast a synthesis may be designated a Being, then that Being is so complex, so all-inclusive as to be beyond the comprehension of the human mind and beyond the possibility of restriction to any single form; for the idea of God includes Everlasting Law, Everlasting Will, Everlasting Life, Everlasting Mind.

In manifestation, "God" is objectively active. In non-manifestation, "God" is quiescent. Behind both activity and quiescence is THAT which is eternal and unchanging, the Absolute, Self-Existent Self. The Creative Agent referred to by various names in the world's cosmogonies is the active expression of that eternal, incomprehensible One Alone.

The names "God" and "Logos" are thus used in this book to connote a Divine Being, omnipresent as the Universal Energising Power, Indwelling Life and Directing Intelligence within all substance, all beings and all things, separate from none. This Being is manifest throughout the Solar System as Divine Law, Power, Wisdom, Love and Truth, as Beauty, Justice and Order.

The Solar Logos is regarded as both immanent within and transcendent beyond His [1] System, of which He is the

---

[1] In this case, also, the masculine is used for convenience only, the Divine Principle—in no sense a Person—being regarded as equally masculine, feminine and androgyne. Father, Mother and Son in one Supernal Power.

threefold "Creator", Sustainer and Regenerator of all worlds and the Spiritual Parent of all beings.

Whether as Principle or Being, God has been conceived in many aspects and as playing many roles. Ancient Egyptian, Hellenic, Hebrew, Hindu and Christian Cosmogonies represent Him as bringing His worlds into existence by means of the creative power of sound. In Christianity we are told: "In the beginning was the Word, and the Word was with God, and the Word was God." [1] Then God spake and in six creative epochs or "days", each followed by a period of quiescence or "night", all worlds, all kingdoms of Nature and all beings came into existence. As a result of this outpouring of creative energy as sound, forms appeared expressive of the divine creative Intent, embodiments of divine Life and vehicles for divine Intelligence. Thus God may be conceived as Celestial Composer, Divine Musician, perpetually composing and performing His creative symphony, with its central theme and myriad variations. This concept of creation by the Voice, known as the Logos doctrine, important in the study of the subject of the Gods, is developed in later Chapters of this book.

God has also been poetically and mystically described as Divine Dancer. Nature—with all its varied rhythmic motions, including the cyclic swing of planets round the sun, terrestrial changes, the flow of river, waterfall and stream, the ceaseless movement of the ocean waves, the swaying of the trees and flowers, the ever-changing forms of fire and flame, the motions of electrons around their nuclei—is conceived, notably in Hinduism, as part of the great dance of the Supreme by which all things are created and sustained.

Again, God is variously portrayed, as Dramatist whose stage upon which the drama of life is played is the Solar System; as Weaver, whose many-coloured tapestry, Nature and

[1] *John* I, 1.

all her sons, is woven on the loom of time and space; as Gardener, with the Angelic Hosts as husbandmen, the universe His garden sown with every kind of seed of His own creating, and every one destined to produce its own facsimile of Himself. He further is regarded as Architect and Engineer, Geometrician and Scientist, Magician and Ceremonialist with the universe as a temple of many shrines in which creative rituals are perpetually performed. A still higher conception reveals Him as Spiritual King, Divine Emperor, ruling through His hierarchy of ministers His Solar Empire. All beings are His subjects over whom He presides with all-inclusive knowledge and wisdom all-embracing. All these He is and doubtless far more—Creator, Preserver, Transformer of the universe, Spiritual Parent of all its inhabitants.

"A man's idea of God is that image of blinding light that he sees reflected in the concave mirror of his own soul, and yet this is not in very truth God, but only His reflection. His glory is there, but it is the light of his own Spirit that man sees, and it is all he can bear to look upon. *The clearer the mirror, the brighter will be the divine image.* But the external world cannot be witnessed in it at the same moment. In the ecstatic Yogin, in the illuminated Seer, the spirit will shine like the noon-day sun; in the debased victim of earthly attraction, the radiance has disappeared, for the mirror is obscured with the stains of matter." [1]

THE EVOLUTIONARY PLAN

From these concepts of the Deity there emerges inevitably the idea of a divine purpose, a great plan. That plan is assumed throughout this book to be evolution, but not of form alone. The word "evolution" is herein used to connote a process which is dual in its operation, spiritual as well as

[1] Vide *Isis Unveiled,* H. P. Blavatsky, Vol. I, p. xxiv.

material, and directed rather than purely natural or "blind". This process is understood to consist of a continuous development of form accompanied by a complementary and parallel unfolding of consciousness within the form.

Although man cannot completely know the evolutionary plan from his Superiors, Sages and Spiritual Teachers throughout the ages he learns that the motive is to awaken and bring to fulfilment that which is latent, seedlike, 'germinal. Divine Will, divine Wisdom, divine Intellect and divine Beauty, these are latent in all seeds, Macrocosmic and microcosmic. The apparent purpose for which the universe comes into existence is to change potentialities into actively manifested powers.

On Earth, for example, for each of the kingdoms of Nature there is a standard or ideal which is dual, as is the evolutionary process. The ideal for consciousness in the mineral kingdom is physical awareness and for form, hardness and beauty. For plant consciousness the ideal is sensitivity, capacity to feel, and for the plant form, beauty. For animal consciousness, it is self-consciousness of feeling and thought, and for animal form it is beauty. For man the evolutionary goal is the complete unfoldment and expression of his inherent divine powers—will to omnipotence, wisdom to omnipresence and intellect to omniscience. In the "perfect" man or Adept, these powers are expressed in fully conscious unity, and therefore perfect co-operation, with the Creator of all in the fulfilment of His plan.

Human perfection attained, superhuman ideals present themselves. We as men can but conceive of the nature of these by the aid of analogy and the little that the Supermen Themselves have in these days permitted us to know. We may conceive these ideals to be: to compose and perform perfectly with God the great symphony of creation; to produce and enact with Him the drama of life; to weave with and for

Him, consciously contributing to the perfection of His great design; to till His garden with Him, tending His plants of the fullness of their flowering; to manage as Heads of Departments, the organisation which is His Solar System; to build with Him His temple of the universe and, as Principal Officers, to enact therein great rituals of creation; to serve as Regents and Ministers in the Solar and Planetary Governments through which He, as Solar Emperor, administers His wide dominions beneath the stars. This in part, we may assume, is God's plan for Supermen, and indeed for all, since the attainment of superhumanity is the destiny of all:

> "the one far-off divine event
> towards which the whole creation moves."

CREATION

The emergence and subsequent development of a universe and its contents is regarded in occult science as being less the result of an act of creation, followed by natural evolution, than a process of emanation guided by intelligent Forces under immutable Law. The creation or emergence of universes from nothing is not an acceptable concept, all being regarded as emanating from an all-containing, Sourceless Source. This Source is regarded as triune, consisting of pre-cosmic spirit, pre-cosmic matter and eternal motion. This doctrine is further expounded in Part II of this book.

SEERSHIP

As part of the unfoldment of the human intellect into omniscience, the development occurs at a certain stage of human evolution of the faculty of fully-conscious, positive clairvoyance. This implies an extension, which can be hastened by means of self-training, of the normal range of visual response to include both physical rays beyond the violet and, beyond them again, the light of the superphysical worlds.

The mechanism of supersensual vision and the process of its development are referred to in the descriptive matter accompanying Plate 28. It is important to differentiate between the passive psychism of the medium, and even the extra sensory perception (ESP) of parapsychology,[1] and the positive clairvoyance of the student of Occultism. This latter, completely under the control of the will and used in full waking consciousness, is the instrument of research with which during the past thirty years I have endeavoured to enter and explore the Kingdom of the Gods.

THE GODS

This term is used throughout this book to denote, not the symbolic images to which the title was given by ancient peoples, but hierarchical Orders of Intelligences, quite distinct from man in this Solar System, but who either have been or will be men. Information concerning their immensely varied nature and functions forms the subject matter of the third Chapter of Part I and succeeding Chapters of this book. Part V consists of illustrations and descriptions of various types of Gods, as they have appeared to me when attempting to study them by means of extended vision.

Eastern peoples, as well as numerous members of the Keltic and other naturally psychic races, are familiar with the idea of the existence of the Gods. In the East they are called *devas* [2], a Sanskrit word meaning "shining ones" and referring to their self-luminous appearance. They are regarded as omnipresent, superphysical agents of the Creative Will, as directors of all natural forces, laws and processes, solar, interplanetary and planetary.

For these beings the term "the Gods" is chiefly employed in this work. The Kabbalistic term "Sephira" is used in

[1] See the writings of J. B. Rhine, Ph.D., Professor of Psychology, Duke University, N. Carolina, U.S.A., especially *The Reach of the Mind*, Faber, London, and *The Journal of Parapsychology*.

[2] Pronounced deyvaahs.

Part III. *Deva* occurs occasionally, as does its useful adjective *devic*, which applies equally to Archangels, angels and nature spirits. Certain types of Gods, associated more closely with man than with Nature, are referred to as "angels", the four terms being used synonymously. The three main stages of *devic* development have each their own names. Nature spirits, like animals and birds, are actuated by a group-consciousness shared with others of the same genus. Gods, Sephiras, *devas* and angels, have evolved out of group consciousness into separate individuality, as has man. Archangels, especially, have transcended the limitations of individuality and have entered into universal or cosmic consciousness, as has the Superman or Adept.

*   *   *   *   *

Before proceeding to a fuller consideration of the nature, the functions and the activities of the Gods, I offer an answer to those who quite naturally will ask: "Where is the proof of their existence?" Of concrete, demonstrable proof of the fruits of mystical experience there can be none. Of evidence for mystical states of consciousness, in which supersensual faculties may operate, and for the existence of the superphysical worlds and their inhabitants, there is an abundance. Most universal and enduring of this evidence is the folklore of all nations. Throughout all time of which records exist, men have borne testimony to their perception of forces, phenomena and beings not normally visible. Despite wide separation both in time and space, there is a remarkable resemblance between the myths, the legends and the folklore of the various peoples of the earth. This universality, similarity and persistence through the ages of belief in the Gods and the Kingdom of the Gods is strong evidence, I submit, for the existence of a kernel of reality within that belief, a basis of fact upon which folklore is founded.

Added to this is the testimony of those who have made both a science and an art of the process of self-illumination called in the East "yoga". The followers of this, the oldest and greatest of the sciences, the science of the Soul, aver that extension of visual and auditory power and mastery of the forces, first of one's own nature and then of Nature herself, can be deliberately and consciously achieved. Anyone, they say, who will fulfil the necessary conditions, who will obey laws as certain in their operation as those to which the chemist subscribes in his laboratory, can pierce the veil of matter which normally hides from view the eternal, spiritual realities, as the veil of day conceals the ever-shining stars.

In individual experiment and individual investigation alone is proof to be found. Whilst demonstration is admittedly impossible, test by personal research is not. That test I have attempted to apply, and this book is in part a record of my own findings. Whilst all are entitled to question, only those, I submit, who have similarly experimented and explored, have the right to deny.

CHAPTER II

SCIENCE, ANCIENT AND MODERN

THE ATOM OF SCIENCE

THE pronouncements of some modern scientists concerning the nature and construction of the material universe coincide very closely with the teachings of occult philosophy throughout the ages. The quest for truth, directed in this age by physical scientists, is leading away from the materialistic and towards the transcendental outlook. The mechanistic view of scientific phenomena is being discarded, and the method of explaining them by the construction of models has come to be regarded as a hindrance rather than an aid to understanding. In one generation physical science has turned its back upon the mechanistic view and upon such models. Sir James Jeans states:

"A review of modern physics has shown that all attempts at mechanical models or pictures have failed and must fail. For a mechanical model or picture must represent things as happening in space and time, while it has recently become clear that the ultimate processes of nature neither occur in, nor admit of representation in, space and time." [1]

Within living memory, the foremost men of science were proclaiming that in matter was to be found the promise of life. That dictum has since been reversed. The atom as a material particle has itself been found capable of subdivision. All substance is now said to be composed of discrete units of

[1] *Physics and Philosophy*, p. 175.

electricity of differing polarities, like minute grains of sand. The structure of all atoms is at present regarded as being similar. Their shape can be taken as spherical and their mass is concentrated at their centre. This nucleus is composed of neutrons and protons, the former being neutral or uncharged particles and the latter being charged with positive electricity; it is surrounded by an electrical field formed of a planetary system of negatively charged particles, moving in round or elliptical paths or orbits and called electrons.

The relatively simple concept of the atom, in which all protons and neutrons are in the nucleus and all electrons are outside of it is by no means final. Evidence is appearing for the existence of other elemental particles. Whilst the whole universe is regarded as being composed of atoms and every atom known up to now has consisted of combinations of the above basic particles, other types of particles have been discovered. One of these is the positron or positive electron which has the mass of an electron. The neutron is suspected to be a proton-electron pair, a close combination of protons and electrons. The meson, thought by many to be the agent of cohesion in all substance, has been discovered in cosmic rays.

These discoveries of protons and neutrons in the nucleus are leading directly towards the view of occult science, that all matter is an extremely concentrated, "crystallised" or "frozen" form of energy. The Einstein equation, further evidence for the correctness of which was provided by the atomic bomb, is $E = MC^2$, with E as the energy in ergs, M the mass in grams and C the speed of light in centimetres per second. Sir James Jeans in *Physics and Philosophy*, p. 200, writes:

"For the materialists, space was filled with real particles, exercising on one another forces which were electric or magnetic or gravitational in their nature; these directed the motions of the particles and so were responsible for all the activity of the world. These forces were of course as real as the particles they moved.

" But the physical theory of relativity has now shown that electric and magnetic forces are not real at all; they are mere mental constructs of our own, resulting from our rather misguided efforts to understand the motions of the particles. .It is the same with the Newtonian force of gravitation and with energy, momentum and other concepts which were introduced to help us understand the activities of the world."

Thus, the idea of the structure of matter becomes more and more abstract. The electron itself, for example, is not regarded only as a discrete, spherical body moving in geometrical paths. Another way of picturing particles is as waves which concentrate in volumes corresponding to or centred round the above paths. The concept is rather—strange though it appears to the lay mind—"more analogous to a noise which is spread throughout a certain region . . . a kind of disturbance in the aether, most intense at one spot and diminishing very rapidly in intensity as we move away from this spot." (*The ABC of Atoms*, Bertrand Russell.)

Occult science adds to this the existence of "but one indivisible and absolute Omniscience and Intelligence in the Universe, and this thrills throughout every atom and infinitesimal point of the whole Kosmos. . . . There is design in the action of the seemingly blindest forces." (*The Secret Doctrine*, H. P. Blavatsky, Adyar Edition, Vol. I, p. 320.) "Each particle—whether you call it organic or inorganic—is a life." (p. 305) "The 'breath of Heaven' or rather the breath of Life. . . . is in every animal, in every animate speck and in every mineral atom." (p. 260) This breath of Life is defined as Cosmic Electricity, the Force that formed the universe, the noumenon of such "manifestations as light, heat, sound, adhesion and the 'spirit' of ELECTRICITY, which is the LIFE of the Universe." (p. 195) For the occultist the One Life is an objective reality: "We speak of a septenary scale of manifestation, which begins at the upper rung with the One Unknowable CAUSALITY, and ends as Omnipresent Mind and Life, immanent in every atom of Matter." (p. 196)

UNIVERSAL MIND

The occult teaching of the existence of a Universal, Directive Intelligence receives support from certain men of science, if not from all. Sir James Jeans in *The Mysterious Universe* writes:

"We discover that the universe shows evidence of a designing or controlling power that has something in common with our own individual minds. . . ." (p. 137)

"The Universe can be best pictured . . . as consisting of pure thought, the thought of what, for want of a wider word, we must describe as a mathematical thinker." (p. 124)

"A thought or idea cannot exist without a mind in which to exist. We may say an object exists in our minds while we are conscious of it, but this will not account for its existence during the time we are not conscious of it. The planet Pluto, for instance, was in existence long before any human mind suspected it, and was recording its existence on photographic plates long before any human eye saw it. Considerations such as these led Berkeley to postulate an Eternal Being, in whose mind all objects existed. . . . Modern science seems to me to lead, by a very different road, to a not altogether dissimilar conclusion." (pp. 125-6)

Sir Arthur S. Eddington has stated:

"Something Unknown is doing we don't know what—that is what our theory amounts to. . . . Modern physics has eliminated the notion of substance. . . . Mind is the first and most direct thing in our experience. . . . I regard Consciousness as fundamental. I regard matter as derivative from Consciousness. . . . The old atheism is gone. . . . Religion belongs to the realm of Spirit and Mind, and cannot be shaken."

J. T. Sutherland, writing in *The Modern Review* (of Calcutta) for July, 1936, quotes the following: [1]

Einstein: "I believe in God . . . who reveals Himself in the orderly harmony of the universe. I believe that Intelligence is manifested throughout all Nature. The basis of scientific work is the conviction that the world is an ordered and comprehensible entity and *not* a thing of chance."

J. B. S. Haldane: "The material world, which has been taken for a world of blind Mechanism, is in reality a Spiritual world seen very partially and imperfectly. The *only real* world is the Spiritual world. . . . The truth is that not Matter, not Force, not any physical thing, but Mind, personality, is the central fact of the Universe."

Kirtley F. Mather, geologist, Harvard: "The nearest approach we have thus far made to the Ultimate, in our analysis of Matter and of Energy, indicate that the Universal Reality is Mind."

[1] Quoted from *The Essential Unity of all Religions* (pp. 22, 23 & 24), by Bhagavan Das, M.A., D. Litt., Benares and Allahabad Universities.

Similarly, in psychology the brain is no longer regarded as a satisfactory model of the mind, a mechanism of concrete particles which constitute the whole machinery of thought. The brain is now looked upon by many as an instrument, thought a separate energy which drives it.

Dr. Kennedy's A. Walter Suiter lecture, Buffalo, April 29, 1941, published in the *New York State Journal of Medicine*, October 15th, 1941, contained the following, reproduced in *Main Currents in Modern Thought*,[1] November 1941:

". . . The notion of 'space-empty' or 'space-ethereal' has today been abandoned, and Nature is now viewed as Energy, patterned into Worlds, patterned variously also for every stick, stone, or bit of life upon them. Man thus becomes one with his environment, which pervades him wholly and into which he extends himself hugely; born according to his manner, he holds his unique pattern as a momentary opportunity for experience; a stream of creative continuity, with aim.

"Anywhere where vitality exists, aim is found. A primitive consciousness exists as 'purpose' in every living cell and organized itself as structure; this primitive mind becomes specialized, layer upon layer, super-segment upon super-segment, into complicated reflexes, later more complicated instincts, and later, still more complex emotional tones and feelings, integrated and channelled for expression through thalamus and hypothalamus. Finally, there has been added the neopallium, the new brain, more and more exquisitely integrated—a concatenation of such ordered representation and swift activity that through it primitive power can eventually appear even as the gift of critical discrimination. Slowly, too, this primitive cellular power is distilled into a sense of spatial, and temporal relationship. Up to the present of evolutionary time, the highest product of this captured, specialized, focused Energy of Cosmic Origin is our self-awareness, self-direction, power of surmise, the power of speculative imagination which almost denies the Universe itself for Boundary—all radiated, implemented, and sometimes disturbed, by Emotion.

"Purpose is mediated by protoplasm. Our consciousness is an enormous amplification of early purpose as primitive as tropism,[2] and it is raised to its highest form and focused for its greatest good by the contrivance of symbolism and imagery and the invention of the tool of speech. This distillate of consciousness is thus focused into self-awareness. Such achievement is nothing but the flowering of the aim, drive, and purpose, innate and part and parcel of every cell in our bodies."

Referring again to J. T. Sutherland's article, one finds the following quotations:

[1] F. Kunz, Editor and Publisher, 12 Church Street, New Rochelle, (New York 10805, U.S.A.)

[2] The phenomenon observed in living organisms of moving toward or away from a focus of light, heat or other stimulus.

Robert A. Milliken, physicist, Institute of Technology, Pasadena: "God is the *Unifying Principle* of the universe. No more sublime conception has been presented to the mind of man, than that which is presented by Evolution, when it re-presents Him as revealing Himself, through countless ages, in the age-long inbreathing of life into constituent Matter, culminating in man with his Spiritual nature and all his God-like powers."

Sir James Arthur Thomson (*The Great Design*:) "Throughout the World of Animal Life there are expressions of something akin to the Mind in ourselves. There is, from the Amoeba upwards, a stream of inner, of subjective life; it may be only a slender rill, but sometimes it is a strong current. It includes feeling, imagining, purposing, as well as occasionally thinking. It includes the Unconscious."

Of the nature and origin of these forces science as yet says little, but the movement of scientific thought is away from the concrete and towards the abstract. · This is parallel with the evolution of human intelligence, the direction of which is through the analytical and concrete towards the development of the faculties of synthesising and abstract thinking. As an illustration of this, the idea is beginning to dawn that time itself is typical of the kind of material of which the physical world is built. In thus probing external phenomena to their depth, the scientist and the mathematician fall back upon symbols and equations as their only means of expressing their discoveries. Solid substance has melted into a shadow. Only mathematical equations and flowing forces remain.

What is the next step likely to be? The latest pronouncements, as indicated by the above quotations, show that certain men of science—admittedly not all—are beginning to postulate mind as the ultimate reality. Sir James Jeans in his book *The Mysterious Universe* also says (the italics throughout being mine):

"To my mind, the laws which nature obeys are less suggestive of those which a machine obeys in its motion than of those which a musician obeys in writing a fugue, or a poet in composing a sonnet. The motions of electrons and atoms do not resemble those of the parts of a locomotive so much as those of the dancers in a cotillion. And if the 'true essence of substances' is forever unknowable, it does not matter whether the cotillion is danced at a ball in real life, or on a cinematograph screen, or in a story of Boccaccio. If all this is so, *then the universe can be best pictured*, although still very imperfectly and inadequately, *as consisting of pure thought, the thought of what, for want of a wider world, we must describe as a mathematical thinker.* (pp. 123, 124)

". . . in the stately and sonorous diction of a bygone age, he (Berkeley) summed up his philosophy in the words:

" 'All the choir of heaven and furniture of earth, in a word all those bodies which compose the mighty frame of the world, have not any substance without the mind. . . . So long as they are not actually perceived by me, or do not exist in my mind, or that of any other created spirit, they must either have no existence at all, or else subsist in the mind of some Eternal Spirit.' " (p. 126)

"Today there is a wide measure of agreement, which on the physical side of science approaches almost to unanimity, that the stream of knowledge is heading towards a non-mechanical reality; *the universe begins to look more like a great thought than like a great machine.* Mind no longer appears as an accidental intruder into the realm of matter; we are beginning to suspect that we ought rather to hail it as the creator and governor of the realm of matter—not of course our individual minds, but the mind in which the atoms out of which our individual minds have grown exist as thoughts. . . .

"*We discover that the universe shows evidence of a designing or controlling power that has something in common with our own individual minds—* not, so far as we have discovered, emotion, morality, or, aesthetic appreciation, but the tendency to think in the way which, for want of a better word, we describe as mathematical. And while much in it may be hostile to the material appendages of life, and also is akin to the fundamental activities of life; we are not so much strangers or intruders in the universe as we at first thought. Those inert atoms in the primeval slime which first began to foreshadow the attributes of life were putting themselves more, and not less, in accord with the fundamental nature of the universe." (pp. 137, 138)

This, if the concept be added of individual Intelligences, Archangelic and angelic embodiments of the "great thought", might well have been written by an exponent of occult philosophy. It is, however, but just to quote also Sir James Jeans's further words, "that everything that has been said and every conclusion that has been tentatively put forward, is quite frankly speculative and uncertain". (p. 138)

THE SOURCE OF KNOWLEDGE

The position of the occultist, on the other hand, is somewhat different. The age-old teachings of occult science are founded, not upon speculations but upon the continually repeated, direct observations of highly trained occult investigators. With the inner eye itself fully operative and the technique of its use fully developed as a result of training under their Adept seniors in evolution, these seers perceive direct the phenomena of Nature on all planes of existence and corroborate the findings of their brother seers who have gone before. For this reason, "to the Occultists who believe in the knowledge acquired by countless generations of Seers and Initiates, the data offered in the Secret Books are all sufficient ".[1]

The assertions of occult science are "made on the cumulative testimony of endless series of Seers who have testified to this fact. Their spiritual visions, real explorations by, and through psychical and spiritual sense untrammelled by blind flesh, were systematically checked and compared one with the other, and their nature sifted. All that was not corroborated by unanimous and collective experience was rejected, while that only was recorded as established truth which, in various ages, under different climes, and throughout an untold series of incessant observations, was found to agree and receive constantly further corroboration.

"The methods used by our scholars and students of the psycho-spiritual sciences do not differ from those of students of the natural and physical sciences. Only our fields of research are on two different planes, and our (Theosophical) instruments are made by no human hands, for which reason, perchance, they are only the more reliable." [2]

Even so, such teachings of occult science as are offered to the general public are invariably presented as ideas for consideration, and never as dogmas representing final truths. Above all things, free enquiry is insisted upon by those who practise and teach the methods of occult science.

[1] *The Secret Doctrine*, H. P. Blavatsky, Adyar Edition, Vol. IV, p. 269.
[2] *The Key to Theosophy*, H. P. Blavatsky, Abridged Edition, pp. 45, 50.

CHAPTER III

CREATIVE PROCESSES

THE MINERAL KINGDOM

THE manner of the original creation or physical formation of mineral substances, whether crystalline and capable of crystallisation or amorphous (colloidal) is as yet unknown to science. In offering the results of attempted observations of the process. I do not for a moment presume to have solved this problem. If what follows is of any worth, it may perhaps be regarded as the observations of a single onlooker which may later be found to have some validity.

The existence of physical agencies is partly, but not wholly, sufficient to account for the appearance of minerals. They are known to be functions of heat and pressure in certain ratios and aqueous vapours, but why a substance crystallises, generally into a characteristic geometrical form or molecular arrangement, is, as yet, unknown. Crystals of regular design always appear when a solution of substance is allowed to evaporate and the same substance usually assumes the same crystal form, *e.g.* salt in cubes, alum in octahedra, nitre in prisms. The term growth is applied to minerals, but this is not regarded as being the result of the addition of newly formed substance but rather of the activity of external agencies which change the contents. The majority of crystalline minerals pre-existed and were gradually deposited in rocks by percolating water or from the molten state as the earth cooled down.

THE LOGOS DOCTRINE

One part of the explanation offered by Theosophy consists of one aspect of what is called the Logos Doctrine. In one sense, and as far as my understanding goes, this implies the emission of a formative or shape-producing electro-spiritual energy—the noumenon of physical electricity—of the order or quality of sound, a soniferous creative force or Word, a creative chord. In terms of frequency of oscillation, the notes of this chord are expressive of the component ideas of an archetype pre-conceived and held in the major Creative Mind throughout *Manvantara*.[1] This archetypal idea partly serves as a dynamic model in the superphysical worlds for the shaping of etheric and physical matter into the conceived pattern. This is the source of the impulse which causes inorganic and organic substance to assume geometrically-governed forms and of the organising, pattern-assuming characteristic of protoplasm.

THE BUILDERS

My own observations suggest that the form-producing process is aided by the actions of Hierarchies of Creative Intelligences—Archangels and their angel hosts—who, as embodiments of Universal Intelligence, know the design or archetypes and, by allying themselves with the Word-force, enhance or amplify its formative capacity. These Beings live in the superphysical worlds and act perpetually as form-moulding agencies, according to the Word. It should be understood that the terms spiritual and superphysical do not imply spatial separation from the physical universe. Matter at every degree of density co-exists spatially, the finer

[1] See footnote 2, p. 24.

interpenetrating the denser. The laboratory of Nature and its "engineers", "artists" and "chemists" are *within* physical substance, somewhat as Hertzian waves are transmitted through the air and an electrical current along a wire. Both protyle [1] and protoplasm are "charged" from within by an indwelling, immanent, thought-directed, creative, formative Life-force.

At the etheric-physical level, the Hierarchies of Creative Intelligences are represented by the minor builders of form, the nature spirits, the Sephiroths in miniature, who operate instinctually, largely by playing along the lines of force—stimulating to them—which form the geometrical patterns set up in the all-pervasive ether by the emitted and vibrating THOUGHT-WORD-FORCE.

THE "WORD"

In Chapter I the concept was presented of the Logos as Musician and the continuous process of creation as the performance of a great symphony. This, "the Great Work", He conceived and developed in earlier creative "Days", [2] and perchance perfected it in the silence and darkness of intermediate, creative "Night". When once more there is to be light, He "speaks" and by the power of His "Word" brings all things into being. This first expression of the "motif" of the new universe is "heard" or responded to by virgin matter, and the planes of Nature with their forms and inhabitants gradually appear. Into these the Logos pours forth perpetually His Life that they may live, this being His continuous sacrifice, His everlasting oblation.

The Logos or *Verbum* is, in reality, no word or voice of any Being. It is pure Will expressive of the presumed

---

[1] Primal substance.

[2] According to occult philosophy, Solar Systems in obedience to a universal, cyclic law emerge, pass into obscuration and re-emerge perpetually. Each new "creation" continues the evolutionary process from the stage attained at the close of the preceding era. These periods of obscuration and manifestation are known as "Nights" and "Days", in Sanskrit *Pralayas* and *Manvantaras*.

purpose or intent of the divine Father-Mother in bringing forth the Universe. It is the irresistible, all-pervasive, inherent impulse to self-expression, expansion (hence the name of Brahma, from the Sanskrit word *brih*, to expand and grow) and fullness which reigns at the heart of all Nature and all Creation from the highest to the lowest. It is the will to fullness which "sounds forth" at that Cosmic moment when divine Ideation is first emanated as Will-Light from the Absolute.

Throughout the Cosmic Days and Years which follow, that Will-Light calls into existence suns, planets, beings, in obedience to law. Level after level and plane after plane of increasing density come into existence and gradually embody and show forth the Will-Light. Monads flash forth their Rays. Beings are emanated and inhabit the planes. Deeper and deeper penetrates the Cosmic Will-Thought-Word, awakening the sleeping substance, forcing its atoms to answer, to embody and echo, or re-sound, the Cosmic Word. The Light shines forth from the Centre to illumine the darkness and render visible the hitherto invisible robes in which the All-Mother is enwrapped.

The Will becomes more potent. The Sound of the Word becomes louder and the Light becomes brighter as the Aeons pass. The Monads become more radiant and their forth-flashed Monadic Rays wider and more brilliant. The denser regions assume the intended forms. The outer darknesses give way to Light, and where once there was Chaos, divine Order rules.

In each and every being thus called into existence as dweller and toiler in the created worlds, the Cosmic processes are, microcosmically, reproduced and fulfilled in parallel. As the whole responds so does every part. In man, as one such dweller and toiler in the worlds, the inertia and silence inherent in matter give place to rhythmic motion and to the "heard" and "answered" creative Voice. In man, as in universe, darkness is displaced by light.

The universal "Word" when uttered becomes manifest as myriads of chords, each a coherent, self-existent sound with its force and light manifestations. Each chord appears as a relatively changeless, abstract form, Archetype or divine idea, in the higher worlds of each of the planets. These Archetypes in their turn sound their "word", "relaying" into the lower worlds the primal Word-force. Magnetic fields are set up therein, matter is drawn into them and, with the aid of the Gods, is moulded into evolving forms. These forms, vivified by divine Life, become the abode of intelligences (the Monads) at the mineral, plant, animal, human and superhuman phases of development. As a result of experience in the forms, these intelligences, assisted by the Gods, gradually unfold their innate faculties and powers until the degree of development set both for them and for the forms has been attained. The Gods are thus conceived both as builders of form and assistants in the evolution of consciousness.

When this standard has been reached by all beings and, in obedience to the law of cycles, the time limit of objective manifestation has been attained, the whole Solar System is withdrawn into the subjective state. In this condition it remains until under the same cyclic law it reappears and the process of development or ascent is continued from the point reached at the close of the preceding period of objective manifestation. Occult philosophy sees this process as continuing indefinitely, there being no limit to the evolutionary possibilities. This orderly progression has no conceivable beginning and no imaginable end.

CREATIVE HIERARCHIES

The creative energies of which all forms are the product, first emitted as sound by the utterance of the "Word", may be thought of as arising from a central, spiritual Source, represented physically by the sun. At their source, these energies have tremendous potency. The whole race of the Gods from the Solar Archangels to the planetary angels serve somewhat as electrical transformers. They receive into themselves the primordial, creative power, and as if by resistance to its flow reduce its "voltage". From the Solar Gods it passes through their lesser brethren, rank upon rank, until it reaches the physical worlds. There, with the assistance of the nature spirits, it throws matter into shapes conceived by the Creative Mind.

The capacity of sound to produce forms may perhaps find support from sonorous figures which can be formed by the vibrations of substance emitting a musical tone. Geometrical figures are, for example, formed by sand on a plate of glass

FIG. 1

or metal when the bow of a violin is drawn along the edge. Ernst Florens Friedrich Chladni (1756-1827), a German physicist, produced geometrical acoustic figures which were formed by the nodal lines in a vibrating plate, made visible by sprinkling sand on a plate, where it settles on the lines of least resistance. Jules A. Lissajous, a French scientist

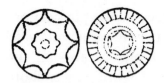 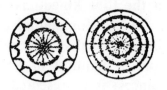

FIG. 2

(1822-1880), produced figures formed by curves due to the combination of two simple harmonic motions. They are commonly exhibited by the successive reflections of a beam of light from the prongs of two tuning forks or by the mechanical tracing of the resultant motion of two pendulums as in a harmonograph, or by means of Wheatstone's rods. Lissajous also produced figures given by a horizontal and a vertical tuning fork vibrating simultaneously. The figures differ when the forks are either in unison or at varying differences of phase and of notes apart. If the capacity of physical sound to produce forms may also be attributed to sonorous creative energy or Word-force emitted at superphysical levels, then the Logos Doctrine finds some scientific support.

The Order of the Gods who thus assist the Logos in the process of the production of evolving forms by the utterance of the "Word", are known as the Builders. The members of the higher ranks of this Order—one race of which is known in Hinduism as the *Gandharvas* or Gods of Music [1]—are aware of the creative intent, perceive and know the Archetypes or divine ideas. By self-unification with the descending Word-force, particularly with such streams as are vibrating at frequencies which are identical with those of their own nature, they amplify them and consequently augment their form-producing power. For within the Order of the Builders are hierarchies which are manifestations of those chords in the creative "Word" of which the Archetypes and forms are expressions. This affinity of vibration draws the particular hierarchy into its appropriate field of work as form-builders in the four kingdoms of Nature.

Gold, for example, may be regarded as the physical product of creative energy vibrating at the frequency at which gold is manifest in terms of force. Gold, as also all substances, is represented in the creative "Word" as a chord, which is the expression in terms of sound of the divine idea of gold. This Word-force is emitted from the spiritual Source and, impinging upon virgin matter, by processes previously described, causes it physically to assume the typical molecular arrangement and crystalline form of gold.

[1] See Plate 20 and accompanying description.

THE GODS OF GOLD

This process is not purely automatic. There is a hierarchy of Gods, the chord of whose nature is identical with that of gold. They may be thought of as the divine idea of gold manifest as an Order of living beings. Members of this hierarchy are drawn by vibratory affinity into the streams of gold force which are constantly descending from the creative Source into the physical world. Their presence and assistance intensify the component frequencies and thereby augment the form-producing power of the Word-force. Thus, part of the function of the Gods of gold, as also of all Gods of the Order of the Builders, is to assist in the process of the production of physical substances and forms. [1]

On the surface of such a gold-bearing reef as the Witwatersrand in South Africa, I have seen numbers of Gods and nature spirits associated with the creative force, the ensouling life and the indwelling consciousness of gold. Above them both spatially and in evolution, were groups of higher Gods, whilst beyond these again, dimly perceived, was the one planetary Intelligence of Gold. This great Being appeared to be merged, as Co-ordinator, Director and Awakener, with the force, the life and the consciousness of Gold.

On the Rand, at the levels of emotion and concrete thought, a Gold group consciousness exists. This is separated from other mineral groups by its enveloping membrane, the differences of the frequency of gold creative force and the fact of the superior development of the ensouling life of gold. The descending force, if described diagrammatically rather than actually, or from a three-rather than a four-dimensional viewpoint, resembles roughly a glowing, conical shaft of sunlight shining from the apex which is the planetary creative Source, down into the earth. The life within the stream is more highly coloured and more awake than that of any other

[1] See Plate 18.

mineral in this region. Attuned to its frequency or rhythm, I felt its power playing through my own bodies, arousing, stimulating all that corresponds to gold in the human constitution.[1]

The hosts of the Gods of gold were seen moving amidst the descending stream of gold power. As shown on Plate 18, these are somewhat feminine in appearance. The face gives the impression of a very pale, almost colourless skin. The "hair"—in reality streaming force—is flaxen with a glint of gold. The aura sweeps down in flowing curves, widening as it descends in bands of very soft shades of leaf green, rose, yellow and delicate blue. The lower third of the aura is filled with myriads of points of gold light. These are all in rapid motion and grow more and more numerous towards the "hem" of this lovely auric robe. The whole form and aura of the God—or Goddess—shine brilliantly with the sheen of gold.

These lesser Gods of gold are curiously impassive. Occasionally those near the surface of the veldt move slowly in a chainlike interweaving, as of a movement in some stately dance. At the same time they maintain a graceful motion of the arms, as in the hand-sowing of seed. Apparently oblivious of externals, they use their minds to impart to the "descending" triple stream of gold power, life and consciousness an additional force and individuality. Even if the attention of one of them is caught and held, it sees one but dimly as if through a gold mist and makes no effort to respond.

Various types of nature spirits are down in the depths, often a mile below. Some have weird, satyr-like bodies— etheric relics of Nature's unaided efforts to build forms in earlier cycles—with long, thin, pointed faces and nude, swart bodies of human shape, save that the legs and feet resemble those of some animal. Each is associated with a certain area

[1] All life, force, substance, potentiality, exist in man, who is a microcosm, an epitome of the Macrocosm, a synthesis of the whole universe. Vide Chapter IV, and *The Secret Doctrine*, H. P. Blavatsky, Vol. V, p. 421, Adyar Edition.

of subterranean rock. They appear to be manipulating earth forces, using tremendous will-power in the process, as if they were hammering and welding the descending energies into homogeneity and solidarity. This work is, however, not manual but the result of instinctively exerted will. They seem to gain great satisfaction from this activity, to experience a feeling of mastery over powerful forces which gives them the impulse to sustain their concentration.

The gold appears amongst the rock like tiny beads, whilst the smallest gold nature spirits moving around and within them resemble minute bacteria of spiral form, in colour glowing gold. At the etheric level, myriads of them are "swimming" about in the descending stream where the deposits occur. The whole gives the impression of a vast laboratory with innumerable workers, in which elements are continually being formed and over which a Mastermind presides.

The Gods and nature spirits of gold do not appear to resent the mining. They are utterly impersonal and wherever the gold is taken they are in contact with the life within it. Similarly the rock gnomes do not resent rocks being broken up. On the contrary, explosions and drilling stimulate them and they revel in the display of power, not caring that the rock is shattered. Indeed, they are less aware of the solid rock than of the force compressed within it. They can see the boring tools but are not normally aware of men, being so remote in terms of frequency from man that they are almost blind to human existence. They regard their own participation somewhat as a great game which they enjoy because it stimulates them to added awareness and increased activity.

CREATION IN THE PLANT KINGDOM

As far as my observations go, similar creative processes occur in the organic kingdoms of Nature. The problems

connected with organic life are profound and, as when referring to the formation of minerals, I do not presume to offer
final solutions of them. It is admitted that chemical characteristics alone do not constitute living, organic material.
Life is presumed to be present, but it has up to now eluded
scientific research. The various processes of biological organisation leading to the development of form, such as progression from a fertilised egg to the adult plant or animal, are
as yet a profound enigma.

Some of the machinery of this progression has been discovered. Genes and chromosomes control development to
some extent and step into the process at the right time and
place, but the emergence of the form of a body from the fertilised seed appears to demand the operation of a designing and
co-ordinating mind; for regulatory activity is shown in all
types of biological organisation arising in a series of orderly
steps from the mysterious substance known as protoplasm.
The form of the body is assumed to be immanent in the fertilised egg, but how that which is latent becomes objective is,
as yet, unknown. Under the microscope, a section of a group
of cells from which a plant or fruit will develop looks like a
chaos of dividing cells. Nevertheless, each cell has its particular task in the combination and the whole organism is part
of a patterned system.

CELL GROWTH

A living cell is able to store up energy which leads to
growth and the process of reproduction. Simple materials,
unlike themselves but of the same atomic structure, are absorbed as food. Plant cells absorb carbon dioxide, for example, and under photo-synthesis can build up carbohydrates.
A crystal, however, only grows in material which is the same
as itself. The more evolved condition than in minerals of
the indwelling life of plants is also indicated by the ability of

living organisms to react to external stimuli, such as sunlight, and to display powers of self-preservation or maintenance of identity and integrity, and by observed behaviour.

The presence of this indwelling and evolving life is so far undetectable by science but not necessarily by the higher senses of man. It is, however, being regarded as a logical necessity in view of the behaviour of living matter. Whether this life essence universally distributed throughout space is called "cosmoszoa" or "panspermia", under right conditions it plays its essential part in giving rise to living matter. In addition, the cell grows by the deposit of electrically-charged particles or ions. Charged molecules are deposited in correct balance so that perfect development may take place for the particular organism.

GENES AND CHROMOSOMES

The processes of germination, cell division and specialisation according to types of structure to be built are thought to occur partly as a result of self-energising processes. Within the seed, minute bodies, called genes, transmit hereditary qualities. These contain an enzyme system and act as organisers which give birth to particular functions of the total form which is to grow. These processes are initiated as a result of adequate stimulation such as the union of the positive and the negative germ cell. This then starts to divide without an initial increase in size. Thereafter, different types of cells begin to evolve in order to produce different types of tissue. After a certain phase, an increase of substance from outside occurs and this is organised into types according to the structure and function of the organism-to-be. A shaping, formative agency produces changes in the energy relationships within the structure affecting the speed of division of the cells, the metabolic rate and the chemical constitution of individual types of cells. All this occurs according to the

Anlagen (German, prototype) of organs which will later be formed.

REGENERATION

The processes of regeneration are as mysterious as those which bring about the original formation from protoplasm. A plant, for example, will regenerate roots if the shoot is cut off. If a young animal embryo is divided into two cells and one of them is killed, the remaining one will develop into a whole animal. The head end of an earthworm which has been cut in two will grow a new tail and the giant sequoia will rebuild trunk tissue after having been burned almost to a shell. Both growth and regeneration are clearly occurring under control according to a characteristic design.

The control consists, says Theosophy, of an indwelling, universal directing Intelligence containing, if not wholly consisting of, the thought of the universe and all it will ever produce, reproduce, generate and regenerate at all stages of growth and throughout every phase of evolutionary development. Progression according to pattern or organised assumption of characteristic forms, stage by stage, is produced or established as a function of protoplasm by the agency of an emitted, form-producing electrical potency, in some ways similar to that of sound. This form-producing energy, originally emitted at superphysical levels and frequencies by the Universal Mind as Emanator and Architect of the universe, is inherent and active within matter itself, and so within protoplasm, bestowing upon it its impulse and capacity progressively and timelessly to produce patterned cell changes to the end of the construction of cell-built types of tissue. As elsewhere described, embodiments of this Universal Mind, certain Hierarchies of Angelic Hosts, assist in these processes.

Occult science thus teaches that nothing which exists is truly inanimate. Life is present in the mineral as in all other forms. Every seed, and especially every germ, is informed or ensouled by a vital energy which causes it to germinate and develop according to its species.

THE CALL TO THE NATURE SPIRITS

A living centre which contains the stored-up results of the previous season as a vibratory possibility is in the heart of every seed. The seasonal awakening or stirring to life in an appropriate soil produces a subtle equivalent to "sound". This "sound" is then "heard" in the elemental regions surrounding its source and the nature spirit builders answer the call. Every type of growth—stem, shoot, leaf and flower—has its own note or call, to which the appropriate builder responds. As sound itself has a form-producing effect, it is the means by which the archetypal form of the plant, latent in the seed and in the minds of a superior order of nature spirits, is projected to the etheric level as a patterned shape. Some of the results of this vibratory call from the seed are:

(1) To separate and insulate the atmosphere around the seed.
(2) To set the matter within the insulated space vibrating at the required rate, and to specialise it in readiness for the work of the nature spirit builders.
(3) To call the builders who, entering the specialised sphere, are then able to materialise themselves down to the level at which they have to work.
(4) To assist in shaping an etheric pattern or mould of the plant as a guide or a ground-plan, ready for the builders.

Different vibrational "cells" arise, as stem, shoot, leaf and flower have in turn to be built and the corresponding builders then arrive to work at their own appropriate task.

The subtle sound appears to radiate not only from the life centre of the seed, but also from every embryo cell as each develops. The builder concerned with that cell absorbs the material required—that which responds to the same vibration as itself and the cell it is building—and transforms it by changing it from free to specialised material. This substance then passes to the cell from which the sound is uttered and is built into the etheric pattern. The cell is thus gradually nourished and enlarged till it reaches its proper limit, when it divides and the process is repeated. While the material is in close association with the builder it is not only specialised to suit the growing cell; it is also coloured by the vibratory rate of the tiny nature spirit concerned.

When examining bulbs growing in bowls, I have seen large numbers of these microscopic, etheric creatures moving in and around the growing plants. They are visible at the etheric level as points of light playing around the stem and passing in and out of the bulb. They absorb matter from the surrounding atmosphere, which they deposit on re-entering the tissues, and this process goes on continuously until the plant is full-grown. The creatures are entirely self-absorbed and sufficiently self-conscious to experience a dim sense of well-being and even of affection for the plant. When outside of it and absorbing matter, they become enlarged and look like pale violet and lilac-coloured spheres about two inches in diameter. Having expanded to the largest size of which they are capable they return and, as stated above, re-enter the plant, into which they discharge the matter and vital force which they have absorbed.

In addition to this, the plants themselves can be seen to take in directly a certain amount of substance from the atmosphere. There is also a natural outflow of vital energy from the half-grown plants to about two feet above and all around them and in this other tiny creatures play and dance. The nature spirit builders do not confine their work to one plant or even to one bowl; for when bowls are near each other, they flit about from one to the other. The bulbs themselves give the impression of being small power houses, each charged with potent forces. The etheric colour of the bulb when growing is pinkish-violet, with an intenser light in the centre, from which rises an upward-flowing etheric stream, carrying with it, at a slower pace, both physical moisture and nutriment.

Each change in structure and colour calls for another group of builders and when the bulb begins to be formed, an appropriate order of nature spirits arrives on the scene. When the flower itself begins to be built, the fairies proper appear, and they are responsible for all the colouring and the structure of the bloom. Flower fairies are sufficiently aware of their special work to take a keen pleasure in its performance. They remain in close attendance as each bud and petal develops and appear to be appreciative of human admiration of the results of their labours. When flowers are cut, the fairy builders may accompany the blooms and stay with them for some hours. By the time the bloom is fully out, the creative chord or "Word" of the plant is fully sounding forth. All the appropriate nature spirits are then present and at work.

Similarly, everywhere throughout Nature, all substances and all forms owe their existence to the ever-uttered, creative "Word" and to the activity of the nature spirits and the Gods. When we look upon Nature's varied forms, her metals and jewels, her flowers, trees and forests, her rivers, lakes and falls, her oceans, her hills and mountain ranges, we are gazing indeed not only upon the materialised auras of the Gods but, if with all reverence one may say so, upon God Himself. For Nature is but God revealed, God's dream made manifest by the continued utterance of His "Word", the chant of His mighty Name, and the ceaseless constructive and beautifying ministry of the greater and lesser Gods. By these, and doubtless by many other means, He brings into existence all beings and all things and sustains them by the perpetual sacrificial outpouring of His Life.

CHAPTER IV

MAN THE MICROCOSM

"THE UNIVERSE IS A MAN ON A LARGE SCALE"[1]

WE may now proceed to study these form-building processes as they are carried out by angels and nature spirits in the construction of the physical, etheric and superphysical bodies of man. In both Nature and man the creative forces, agents and methods are, in general, very much the same. Perhaps the most profound of all the profound truths contained within the esoteric teachings are those of the unity of the Macrocosm or "Great Man" with the microcosm or individual man, and of the close similarity between the processes by which both become manifest and evolve. Man, in very truth, was created in the image of God. "The mystery of the earthly and mortal man is after the mystery of the supernal and immortal One."[2] The universe is the manifestation of a Supreme, Deific Power, a ray of which is present in every man. Realisation of this presence as the true human individuality, the real Self, behind the bodily veil leads to the further realisation that this Dweller in the Innermost is itself forever at one with the Supreme Lord, the eternal Source of light and life and power.

H. P. Blavatsky refers to this unity and similarity in her monumental work, *The Secret Doctrine*:[3]

[1] Lao-Tze.
[2] Eliphas Levi, *Clef des Mystères*.
[3] *Op. cit.*, Vol. V, pp. 421, 429, Adyar Edition.

"To the learner who would study the Esoteric Sciences with their double object: (*a*) of proving Man to be identical in spiritual and physical essence with both the Absolute Principle and with God in Nature; and (*b*) of demonstrating the presence in him of the same potential powers as exist in the creative forces in Nature—to such a one a perfect knowledge of the correspondences between Colours, Sounds, and Numbers is the first requisite. . . . It is on the thorough knowledge and comprehension of the meaning and potency of these numbers, in their various and multiform combinations, and in their mutual correspondence with sounds or words, and colours or rates of motion (represented in physical science by vibrations), that the progress of a student in Occultism depends."

"These seven senses of ours correspond with every other septenate in Nature and in ourselves. Physically, though invisibly, the human Auric Envelope (the amnion of the physical man in every age of Life) has seven layers, just as Cosmic Space and our physical epidermis have. It is this Aura which, according to our mental and physical state of purity or impurity, either opens for us vistas into other worlds, or shuts us out altogether from anything but this three-dimensional world of Matter.

"Each of our seven physical senses (two of which are still unknown to profane Science), and also of our seven states of consciousness—*viz.*: (1) waking; (2) waking-dreaming; (3) natural sleeping; (4) induced or trance sleep; (5) psychic; (6) super-psychic; and (7) purely spiritual—corresponds with one of the seven Cosmic Planes, develops and uses one of the seven super-senses, and is connected directly, in its use on the terrestro-spiritual plane, with the cosmic and divine centre of force that gave it birth, and which is its direct creator. Each is also connected with, and under the direct influence of, one of the seven sacred Planets."

Thus the Logos and man are not only one in essence but all that is in the Logos, which includes the Solar System, is innate in man. Their constitution is precisely similar, that is to say sevenfold. Man as Monad is also immanent within and transcendent beyond his field of manifestation, his seven principles. The creative power and processes by which a Solar System comes into being also operate in human procreation and subsequent bodily development. Significant, therefore, is the statement that "the proper study of mankind is man". The injunction of the Mystery Schools of old, "Man know thyself", was wise; for when man truly knows himself, he knows all.

MICROCOSMIC CREATION

In partial exposition of these great truths, in this Chapter the descent of the human Ego into incarnation [1] is considered

[1] Vide *Reincarnation, Fact or Fallacy?*, Geoffrey Hodson, T. P. H., Adyar.

and certain clairvoyantly observed processes of pre-natal life, in which angels participate, are described. Before this subject can be adequately presented, however, it is necessary to advance certain Theosophical teachings concerning the superphysical and spiritual nature of man.

Man is described as that being in whom highest spirit and lowest matter are united by intellect. Although this makes of him a triplicity, his constitution is said to be at least sevenfold. At the present stage of human evolution, the seven bodies or principles of man, beginning with the most dense, are stated to be the physical body, vehicle of thought, feeling, awareness, and action in the physical world; the etheric double, the connecting link between the inner and the outer man and the container of the vital energy or *prana* received physically from the sun and superphysically from the spiritual sun; the emotional or astral body, vehicle of desire; the mental body, vehicle of the formal mind and instrument of concrete thought; the higher mental or Causal Body, vehicle at the level of abstract mind of the threefold Spiritual Self, called by the Greeks the Augoeides and frequently referred to as the Ego; the Buddhic Body, vehicle of spiritual intuitiveness; and the Atmic Body, vehicle of the spiritual will. Overshadowing and empowering the whole sevenfold man is the Dweller in the Innermost, the Monad or Divine Spark.

As the Macrocosmic creative process begins with the "Word", so the microcosmic creation of the mental, astral and, later, the etheric and physical bodies of man is initiated by the utterance of the Egoic "Word". At or near the time of conception, the physical permanent atom [1] of the Ego about to incarnate is attached by an angel to the twin cell then formed. The permanent or seed atoms are single, ultimate atoms of the planes of will, wisdom, abstract intelligence,

---

[1] Vide *A Study in Consciousness*, A. Besant, p. 55 *et seq.*, 1938, Adyar Edition, T. P. H., Adyar.

formal thought, emotion and physical matter. At the beginning of the descent of the Monadic Ray into the evolutionary field they are attached to this life-thread or Ray of the Monad, which is thus represented on the third, fourth, fifth (that of both abstract and concrete thought), sixth and seventh planes of Nature, counting from above. The Monad itself is situated on the second plane and obtains communication with the planes below through its life-thread on which the atoms are thus strung.

At the opening of each cycle of rebirth, the microcosmic Word-force or Egoic power, life and consciousness descends down the thread of life connecting the Causal Body with the mental, astral and physical permanent or seed atoms. This triple stream of creative energy vibrates on frequencies expressive of the Egoic Ray [1] or Monadic classification, the evolutionary standing, the qualities of character and consciousness already developed and the *karma*,[2] both happy and unhappy in its outworking. All these are represented as "sounds" in the chord of the Egoic "Word" and modify greatly the parental characteristics transmitted via the mental and astral bodies and the ovum and spermatozoon. This creative power originates microcosmically in the Monad or the one indivisible Self of man, the integral spark within the Parent flame, by which the "Word" is primarily uttered. This Monadic "Word" is in its turn a chord in the Macrocosmic *verbum*.

The Causal or Egoic Body, the permanent vehicle of the Spiritual Self of man, the Augoeides, may be thought of as the microcosmic Archetype; it is the vehicle for and expression of Monadic creative power, tuned or coloured, as stated

---

[1] Vide *The Seven Human Temperaments*, Geoffrey Hodson, T.P.H., Adyar.

[2] *Karma*, Sanskrit. The universal law of cause and effect, which guides unerringly all other laws productive of certain effects along the grooves of their respective causations. This law operates not only during a single life, but throughout successive lives, the conditions and opportunities of which are the exact effects of causes generated in preceding incarnations. Absolute justice is by this law assured to every human being. Cf. *Galatians*, VI, 7.

above, by the products of past experience, both on its own plane and through successive personalities. Thus is constituted the "Word" which the Ego in the Causal Body, as microcosm, utters creatively to initiate a new descent into incarnation.

The permanent atom on each plane, awakened from the relatively static condition of inter-incarnation periods, then becomes the focus for, and the transmitter on that plane of, the relayed Word-force. As centres of the magnetic fields they then set up, the permanent atoms attract the type of matter which is capable of response to the emitted wave lengths. This is especially the case as regards the preponderance of one or other of the primary Rays in Monad and Ego and of the three corresponding *gunas*[1] in matter. Thus, in the very substance of which bodies are built, as also in every other particular, perfect justice is automatically meted out to every individual as regards the mental, emotional and physical equipment with which life's journey is begun.

HOW MAN'S BODIES ARE BUILT

This stage immediately following conception may perhaps be compared to that in Macrocosmic processes at which the "Word" has produced the Archetype, and through that the magnetic centres with their fields, within and round which the planets will later be formed. The principles governing the formation of the mental, astral and physical bodies are the same at the three levels, but in order to present as clear an account of the results of my observations as possible, the process of building the physical body *in utero* will be in part described.

As above stated, at the moment of germination the physical permanent atom is attached by an angel to the

---

[1] The three basic qualities of all matter—activity, inertia and rhythm. **Vide** *A Study in Consciousness*, Annie Besant, T. P. H., Adyar.

newly-formed twin cell. This presence of the permanent atom, vivified by the descending, Egoic, creative energy or microcosmic Word-force, bestows upon the twin-celled organism its ordered, biological impetus, causes it, in fact, to grow according to the "Word".

The creative energy, now emitted into and through the permanent atom and twin cell, is found to produce at least four results:

First, the establishment of a field or sphere of influence within which the building is to occur. This corresponds to the formation of the Ring-Pass-Not of the Solar System in Macrocosmic creation, represents the range of the emitted rays, and serves to insulate an area against the intrusion of foreign vibrations and substances.

Second, the magnetisation or attunement of the matter within this field. The play of creative energy brings surrounding matter into vibrational harmony with the individual about to incarnate.

Third, the production of a form. This form, which might be regarded as the etheric mould into which the physical body will be built, must now be described in some detail, such description delaying reference to the fourth effect of the emitted Word-force. Clairvoyantly examined, the pre-natal etheric mould, which appears very soon after conception, resembles a baby body built of etheric matter, somewhat self-luminous, vibrating slightly, a living being, the etheric projection of the Archetype as modified by *karma*.

Within the etheric mould there is to be seen, in terms of flowing energy or lines of force, each on its own wave length, a sketch plan of the whole body. Every type of tissue-to-be is represented, differing from other types because the energy of which it is an end-product is itself on another frequency. Thus the bony structure, muscular and vascular tissues, the nerves, the brain and other substances, are all represented in

the etheric mould by currents of energy on specific frequencies.

The play of the emitted vibrations on the free surrounding matter may possibly be the factor which causes atoms to
enter into differing molecular combinations to produce various
types of tissue. These molecules are attracted towards the
lines of force and "settle" into their appropriate places in the
growing body by virtue of sympathetic vibration or mutual
resonance. Thus, again, every part of the physical body in
substance and in form exactly fits the incarnating Ego. *Karmic*
deficiencies, which are to work out in terms of malformation,
weakness and disease, are represented in the mould by dis-
sonances, or even breaks in the particular lines of force along
and according to which the tissues are built.

To digress briefly, if this generalisation be at all accurate,
the whole body—as also the Solar System—can be expressed
in terms of frequency, each type of tissue and each organ
having its own wave length, note and colour, these in their
turn varying in states of health and of disease. In perfect
health, every part is in tune and the chord of the human body
perfectly harmonised. In ill-health the opposite exists; there
is a dissonance at some part or other. The chord is out of
tune. The true art of healing, therefore, is that of the restoration of rhythm.

Fourth of the effects of germination is the evocation of
the *devic* builders of form. The class or order of these which
is evoked is also decided by resonance. Thus, nature spirits
of the building order in the immediate neighbourhood, which
are in vibrational attunement with the currents or notes in
Word-force emitted by the reincarnating individual, alone
hear and respond. Arriving on the scene, they enter the
sphere of influence and find themselves in an atmosphere
entirely congenial to them, because ruled by their own inherent chord. They then proceed instinctively to absorb into

themselves, and therefore further to specialise, the free matter, after which they assist in its vibrationally-governed deposit into its appropriate place in the growing structure of the body.

THE MECHANISM OF CONSCIOUSNESS

The building angels at the astral and mental levels, in addition to the supervision of these processes through the instinctive response of the nature spirits to their thought, concern themselves also with the construction and extremely delicate adjustment of the mechanism of consciousness. This consists physically of the body itself, the cerebro-spinal system with the seven nerve and glandular centres, situated at the sacrum, the spleen, the solar plexus, the heart, the throat, and the pituitary and the pineal glands. At the etheric level, the etheric counterparts of these centres and glands, and in addition the etheric *chakras*,[1] must be perfectly adjusted to the physical organs, the health and efficiency of which they govern. Similarly, in the astral and mental bodies the seven *chakras* in their turn must be adapted to the corresponding etheric and physical parts of the mechanism. A sevenfold mode of manifestation in the body, and seven channels through which it can gain experience therein, are thus provided for the Ego by the *chakras* and their corresponding physical centres. These human *chakras* are projections of the seven corresponding vortices in the planetary and Solar Archetypes, and, with *devic* assistance, are produced by the play of Word-force from them through the human Causal Body.

Here, also, numerical principles are involved. Each of the *chakras* has its own specific chord or group of frequencies, colours and numbers of divisions resembling the petals

---

[1] *Chakra*, Sanskrit, a wheel or a circle. A spinning vortex in the etheric, astral, mental and higher bodies of man, each of which has seven *chakras*. Vide *The Chakras*, C. W. Leadbeater, T. P. H., Adyar. The almost anglicised "*chakra*" which is the substantive is used in the text throughout. *Chakram* is the nominative and the accusative singular.

of a flower. Through each there flows a type of energy, life and consciousness, vibrationally in harmony with that chord. When *karma* is favourable to perfect function, the chord of each *chakra* is perfectly harmonised, the seven in tune with each other and with each of the bodies in which they exist, as also with the corresponding centres in the other bodies. Under such conditions perfect health and efficiency of function are assured. When there is dissonance—created by transgressions, mental, emotional or physical and the consequent malformation or distortion of the *chakras*—imperfection of function is the result. The *karma* of disease would seem to operate primarily by disturbing vibrational attunement. A break in the rhythm of descending energies at any level ultimately causes ill-health in the physical body. It would appear, therefore, that *final* healing must come from within the sufferer, from the Ego itself; for from the Ego—the human Archetype—alone is emitted creative, and therefore corrective and curative, energy on groups of frequencies numerically expressive of the ideal form.

In successful spiritual healing, a flood of corrective and vitalising force descends through the Ego and superphysical bodies and their *chakras* into the physical body, sweeping out inharmonious substances, restoring harmony and therefore the free and unimpeded flow of the inner life-force throughout the whole Nature. The Healing Angels carry out their mission largely, but not entirely, by the use of this power, by restoration of the full function of the *chakras* concerned, and on occasion by the actual change of substances in the superphysical, etheric and physical bodies. They also direct a powerful stream of cleansing, vitalising and healing forces from their own auras and other natural reservoirs through the physical, etheric and astral bodies especially, thereby setting up conditions under which the natural processes of elimination and of healing can restore the sufferer to health.

Throughout the pre-natal period and for the whole of the lifetime, Egoic Word-force is continuously emitted through the permanent atoms, the *chakras* and the superphysical and physical bodies. When injury occurs, it is this ever-active, formative power which makes possible the repair and rebuilding of tissue according to the original form. In this process, also, angels and nature spirits play their constructive parts.[1] Thus, up to the moment of death, when the Ego withdraws, the physical body is subjected to the influence of the Egoic "Word". The disordered *post mortem* cell and bacterial activity known as decay is due to the absence of this directive influence of the Ego. As the astral and mental bodies are in their turn laid aside, the "Word" also becomes astrally and mentally silent, the Ego having withdrawn into the subjective condition of creative rest and heavenly bliss.[2] From this, in due course, it awakens. Again the Word-force is emitted and a new incarnation begins.

Since man is an epitome of the Solar System, a microcosmic manifestation of the Macrocosm, close resemblances are found between the creative processes described above and those by which a universe comes into being. In man, the microcosm and Macrocosm meet. This cannot be said of the angels since they do not normally possess etheric and physical bodies; neither is it true of animals who are without the three higher principles of Will, Wisdom and abstract Intelligence. In man, however, the full possibilities of Macrocosmic self-expression are contained. The purpose of his existence is the unfolding from within of his Macrocosmic powers, that he may in his turn attain to the stature of the Logos of a Solar System, "perfect as his Father which is in Heaven is perfect".[3] One might almost assume that since the same

---

[1] Vide *The Miracle of Birth*, Geoffrey Hodson, T. P. H., London.
[2] Vide *The Devachanic Plane*, C. W. Leadbeater, T. P. H., Adyar.
[3] *Matthew*, V, 48.

principles govern Macrocosmic and microcosmic creative processes, repeated incarnation provides the training and practice necessary for man's later Macrocosmic manifestation of creative power.

PART II

DESCRIPTIONS

CHAPTER I

THE GREATER GODS

THE SEPHIROTHAL HOSTS

THE contribution of occult philosophy to the problem of the emanation and constitution of the universe is dual. It consists first of an affirmation of the existence in Nature of a directive Intelligence, a sustaining Life and a creative Will; and second of information concerning the existence, nature and function of those individual embodiments of these three Powers in Nature, called in Egypt and Greece "Gods", in the East *Devas*, and in the West "Angelic Hosts".

Occult philosophy shares with modern science the view that the universe consists not of matter but of energy, and adds that the universe of force is the Kingdom of the Gods. For fundamentally these Beings are directors of universal forces, power agents of the Logos, His engineers in the great creative process, which is regarded as continuous. Creative energy is perpetually outpoured. On its way from its source to material manifestation as physical substance and form, it passes through the bodies and auras of the Gods. In the process it is "transformed", "stepped down" from its primordial potency. Thus the creative Gods are also "transformers" of power.

Highest amongst the objective or fully manifested Gods are the seven Solar Archangels, the Seven Mighty Spirits before the Throne. These are the seven Viceroys of the three-fold Solar Emperor. A planetary Scheme [1] or Kingdom in the new-born universe is assigned to each of the Seven from the beginning. Each is a splendid figure, effulgent with solar light and power, an emanation of the sevenfold Logos, whose Power, Wisdom and Beauty no single form can manifest. These mighty Seven, standing amidst the first primordial flame, shape the Solar System according to the divine "idea". These are the seven Sephiras concerning whom and their three Superiors, the Supernal Trinity, fuller information is offered in Part III. Collaborating with them, rank upon rank in a vast hierarchy of beings, are the hosts of Archangels and angels who "imbue primordial matter with the evolutionary impulse and guide its formative powers in the fashioning of its productions". [2]

The Gods differ from man in that in the present *Maha-Manvantara* [3] their will does not become so markedly differentiated from the One Will. The human sense of separated personality is almost entirely absent in them. Their path of evolution which, in the present Solar System, does not deeply penetrate the physical worlds as does that of man, leads from instinctive to self-conscious co-operation with the One Will. Occult science teaches, however, that in preceding or succeeding periods of manifestation they either have been or will be men. H. P. Blavatsky says:

"The whole Kosmos is guided, controlled, and animated by almost endless series of Hierarchies of sentient Beings, each having a mission to perform, and who—whether we give them one name or another, whether we call them Dhyan Chohans or Angels—are 'Messengers', in the sense only that they are the agents of Karmic and Cosmic Laws. They vary infinitely in their respective degrees of consciousness and intelligence; and to call them all pure Spirits, without any of the earthly alloy 'which time is wont to prey

[1] A septenary system of superphysical and physical planets, seven of which are represented physically by Venus, Vulcan, Jupiter, Saturn, Neptune, Uranus and the Earth. Vide *The Solar System*, A. E. Powell, T. P. H., London.

[2] Vide *The Secret Doctrine*, H. P. Blavatsky, Vol. I, p. 246, Adyar Edition.

[3] *Maha-Manvantara*, Sanskrit. Major *Manvantara* as of Planetary Scheme or Solar System. See footnote 2, p. 24.

upon,' is only to indulge in poetical fancy.   For each of these Beings either *was*, or prepares to become, a man, if not in the present, then in a past or a coming cycle (Manvantara).   They are *perfected*, when not *incipient*, men; and in their higher, less material spheres differ morally from terrestrial human beings only in that they are devoid of the feeling of personality, and of the *human* emotional nature—two purely earthly characteristics.   The former, or the 'perfected,' have become free from these feelings, because (*a*) they have no longer fleshly bodies—an ever-numbing weight on the Soul; and (*b*) the pure spiritual element being left untrammelled and more free, they are less influenced by *Maya* than man can ever be, unless he is an Adept who keeps his two personalities—the spiritual and the physical—entirely separated.   The incipient Monads, having never yet had terrestrial bodies, can have no sense of personality or EGO-ism.   That which is meant by 'personality' being a limitation and a relation, or, as defined by Coleridge, 'individuality existing in itself but with a nature as a ground,' the term cannot of course be applied to non-human Entities; but, as a fact insisted upon by generations of Seers, none of these Beings, high or low, have either individuality or personality as separate Entities, *i.e.*, they have no individuality in the sense in which a man says, '*I am myself* and no one else'; in other words, they are conscious of no such distinct separateness as men and things have on earth Individuality is the characteristic of their respective Hierarchies, not of their units; and these characteristics vary only with the degree of the plane to which these Hierarchies belong; the nearer to the region of Homogeneity and the One Divine, the purer and the less accentuated is that individuality in the Hierarchy.   They are finite in all respects, with the exception of their higher principles—the immortal Sparks reflecting the Universal Divine Flame, individualised and separated only on the spheres of Illusion, by a differentiation as illusive as the rest.   They are 'Living Ones,' because they are the streams projected on the Kosmic screen of Illusion from the ABSOLUTE LIFE; Beings in whom life cannot become extinct, before the fire of ignorance is extinct in those who sense these 'Lives'." [1]

TWO STREAMS OF EVOLVING LIFE

The concept, founded upon occult research, of certain Orders of the Angelic Hosts as creative and directive Intelligences, expressions of aspects of the Divine nature and consciousness, Lords of the subtle elements of earth, water, air and fire and Gods of regions of the Earth, differs in one respect at least from that of certain schools of Christian thought. Investigation does not support the view that angels are deceased human beings.   On the contrary, it reveals that human nature and human character undergo no change whatever immediately after death; that temperament, likes and

[1] Vide *The Secret Doctrine*, H. P. Blavatsky, Vol. I, pp. 318, 319, Adyar Edition.

dislikes, gifts, capacities, and for the most part memory, at first remain unchanged. According to the Bible, angels were in existence before the death of the first man. They were present when sentence was passed upon Adam and Eve, and one was placed with flaming sword "to keep the way of the Tree of Life".[1] There would seem, therefore, to be no scriptural foundation for the belief that death transforms men into angels. Indeed, speaking of man, St. Paul says: "Thou madest him a little lower than the angels." [2]

The Biblical account of the angels as ministers and messengers from God to man, appearing to individuals in times of need, is supported by the teaching of occult philosophy. So, also, is the vision of Jacob at Bethel, in which he saw "a ladder set up on the earth, and the top of it reached to heaven; and behold the angels of God ascending and descending on it".[3] The Order of the angels is hierarchical. On the lower rungs of the angelic ladder of life are the lesser nature spirits, brownies and gnomes, associated with the element of earth; fairies and sylphs with that of air; undines or nereids with water; and salamanders with fire. Above them, as previously stated, are angels and Archangels in an ascending scale of evolutionary stature, reaching up to the Seven Mighty Spirits before the Throne.

Countless in their numbers, innumerable in their Orders and degrees, the Gods dwell in the superphysical worlds, each Order performing its particular task, each possessing specific powers and each presenting a characteristic appearance. The whole constitutes a race of evolving beings at present pursuing an evolutionary pathway which is parallel to that of man, and which with him uses this planet and Solar System as a field of activity and unfoldment.

[1] *Genesis* III, 24.
[2] *Hebrews* II, 7, also *Psalm* VIII, 5.
[3] *Genesis* XXVIII, 12.

THE APPEARANCE OF THE GREATER AND THE LESSER GODS

As will be seen from the descriptions which follow and the illustrations in Part V, the angelic form is founded upon the same Archetype or divine "idea" as is that of man. The outlines, however, are less clearly defined, the bodies less substantial, suggesting flowing forces rather than solid forms. Angels themselves differ in appearance according to the Order to which they belong, the functions which they perform and the level of evolution at which they stand.

Brownies, elves and gnomes appear in Western countries much as are described in folk-lore. In some Eastern and Central and South American countries their forms are more archaic, and even grotesque. Undines or nereids, associated with the element of water, resemble beautiful, and generally unclothed, female figures, femininity being suggested by roundness of form, there being, as far as I have found, differences of polarity but no sex differentiation in the Kingdom of the Gods. Varying in height from a few inches to two or three feet, undines are to be seen playing in the spray of waterfalls, reclining in the depths of deep pools or floating swiftly over the surface of river and lake. Fairies and sylphs, associated with the element of air, generally appear to clairvoyant vision much as represented in fairy-tale. They look like beautiful maidens with brightly-coloured wings, not used for flight since these beings float swiftly or slowly at will, their rosy, glowing forms partly concealed by gossamer, force-built "garments". Salamanders, associated with the element of fire, appear as if built of flame, the form constantly changing but suggestive of human shape, the eyes alight with fiery power. The chin and ears are sharply pointed and the "hair" frequently streams back from the head, appearing like tongues of flame, as the salamanders dive steeply into the flames of physical fires and fly through them.

Variations of these forms are to be seen in different countries of the world and in different parts of the same country. Where unspoilt, and not too highly populated, the countryside of England is rich in fairy life, descriptions being given in Part II, Chapter IV.

THE ABODE OF THE GODS

The Gods know the sun, physical and superphysical, as the heart and source of all power and life within the Solar System. From that heart, the vitalising energies which are the life "blood" of the solar and planetary "body" of the Logos are continually outpoured and withdrawn. In bringing the universe into existence, He, the Solar Logos, "breathes" forth His creative power, which flows to the very confines of His system, causing the material universe to appear. At the end of creative Day, He "breathes" in, His power is withdrawn and the material universe disappears, re-absorbed into THAT from which all came forth. This outbreathing and inbreathing of the solar life and energy is rhythmical. The one major creative "Word" or chord of the Solar System consists of innumerable frequencies, differences of vibratory rate producing differences of substance and form. The great race of the Gods lives and evolves amid this universe of outrushing and returning force.

MOUNTAIN GODS

On a single planet such as our Earth, Solar Archangels and angels are represented by corresponding planetary Gods. In addition to these major creative Intelligences, there are the angels presiding over divisions and areas of the surface of the Earth. They are called Landscape Angels and are partly concerned with creative and evolutionary processes in the mineral and plant kingdoms of Nature. A mountain is a living, evolving organism, a body, as indeed is the whole

Earth, in which the Three Aspects of the Logos are incarnate.
At least three processes are occurring within and about every
mountain: the creation and evolution by the action of the
Divine Will-Thought of atoms, molecules and crystals of
which the mountain is built, the vivification of substance and
form by the indwelling Divine Life and the awakening and
development of the incarnate mineral consciousness. In
each of these, Nature is assisted by hosts of nature spirits and
Gods working under the direction of a responsible Official,
who is the mountain God. When a peak is part of a range,
the whole range in its turn will be presided over by a far more
highly evolved Being of the same Order as the Gods of single
peaks.

The appearance of these Beings is most magnificent, as
is shown in the illustrations in Part V of this book, far from
adequate though they be despite the artist's skill. In height
colossal, often ranging from thirty to sixty feet, the mountain
God is surrounded on every side by outrushing, brilliantly
coloured auric forces. These flow out from the central form
in waves, eddies and vortices, varying continuously in colour,
in response to changes of consciousness and activity. The
face is generally more clearly visible than the rest of the form,
which not infrequently is veiled by the outflowing energies.
The features are always strongly yet beautifully modelled.
The brow is broad, the eyes wide set and ablaze with power
and light. Whilst in man the heart and solar plexus *chakras*
are distinct, in mountain and other Gods they are sometimes
conjoined to form a brilliant force-centre, often golden in
colour, from which many of the streams of power arise and
flow forth. On occasions these streams take the form of
great wings stretched out for hundreds of yards on either side
of the majestic figure.

Whilst all such Gods live their own intensely vivid life
amongst their peers in the higher superphysical worlds, one

part of their attention is almost continuously turned towards the mountain below, into the sleeping consciousness and life of which they continually direct streams of stimulating. quickening force. Occasionally, in order to perform its awakening functions more quickly and effectively, a God will descend deep into the mento-astral double of the mountain, its potent energies unified with the creative forces of which the mountain substance and form are products, its life blended with the indwelling Life and its consciousness one with the incarnate, Divine Mind. After a time it reappears and resumes its station high above the peak.

As stated above the Gods of single peaks are subordinate to a still greater God which, though larger and more brilliant, resembles its subordinates and performs similar functions for the whole mountain range and surrounding landscape. Such great Gods of Nature are not usually interested in man, neither do they display knowledge of human life and modes of thought. Intensely concentrated upon their task, they are generally remote and impassive, even as are the snowclad peaks. Certain of them, however, would seem to have had contact with men in earlier civilisations, to have retained interest in human evolution and to be willing, on occasion, to inspire and advise human individuals and groups responsive to their influence.

MESSAGES FROM THE HEIGHTS

Amongst the many mountain Gods observed in the Sierra Nevada Mountains in California, the two presently described showed interest in and knowledge of man. Of the first of these Gods, I wrote at the time of observation:

The great sphere of his [1] outer aura gleams white as sunlit snow-fields across which he moves majestically. Within the

---

[1] Masculine for convenience only, though the male was suggested in the virility and power of the face, form and influence of this particular God, as indeed of all mountain Gods which I have seen.

white radiance, and partially veiled by it, shine the deep greens of the cypress trees, and within these again the golden glory of the noonday sun. Then glows a rosy light of softest hue, next azure blue and last, all white and radiant, the Godlike form.

The face is moulded in strength, square-jawed and powerful. The "hair" resembles flickering, backward-sweeping flames and in the air above a crown of upward-rushing, radiant energies flashes with the brightly coloured jewels of his thoughts.

An attempt to discover something of the content of his consciousness and, more particular, his views concerning the Gods, visible Nature and the ideal relation of man thereto, produces upon me the impression of the utterance of successive principles, each followed by a profound stillness in which the idea is dwelt upon and assimilated. The God thus seems to "say":

"The globe is a living being with incarnate power, life and consciousness. The Earth breathes. Its heart beats. It is the body of a God who is the Spirit of the Earth. Rivers are as its nerves, oceans great nerve-centres. Mountains are the denser structure of the giant whose outer form is man's evolutionary field, whose inner life and potent energies are the abiding place of the Gods.

"The approach to Nature by modern man is almost exclusively through action and his outer senses. Too few among her human devotees approach her in stillness, with outer senses quieted and inner sense aroused. Few, therefore, discover the Goddess herself behind her earthly veil.

"There is a value in the active life, a power and a beauty in Nature's outer garb. Power far greater, and beauty far deeper, lie beneath her veil, only to be drawn aside by silent contemplation of her hidden life.

"The heart of Nature, save for its rhythmic pulse, abides in silence. The devotee at Nature's shrine must approach her altar reverently and with quiet mind if he would find her beating heart and know the power within the form.

"The doorway of her temple exists and is to be found in every natural form. Contemplation of a single flower may lead the seeker through. A plant displaying Nature's symmetry, a tree, a mountain range, a single peak, flowing river, a thundering cascade—each and all of these will serve the contemplative soul of man as entrance to the realm of the Real wherein Nature's Self abides.

"In contemplation of Nature's outward forms, the doorway to her temple should be approached. Self-identification with her inner Life, deep response to her beauty without and within—these are the means of entry to her inmost Shrine.

"Within, await the High Gods, the timeless Ones, the everlasting Priests, who minister throughout creative Day within the temple, which is the natural world.

"Few, far too few, have found entrance there since Greece became a ruin and Rome fell into decay. The Grecians of old dwelt in simplicity. Complexities had not yet appeared. Human character was direct, human life simple and human minds, if somewhat primitive, attuned to the Universal Soul.

"The wheel revolves. The golden days return. Nature calls again to man who, as he hears, endeavours to respond. Man has passed through the cycle of darkness which followed the decay of Rome. Yet, involved in increasing complexities, he has lost his contact with Nature's hidden life. To regain it, all that dulls the senses, everything gross, everything impure and all indulgence must be left behind. The divine heart of Life must be approached in silent contemplation and single-mindedness; thus only may that heart be found."

A second mountain God whose picture appears on Plate 15, was in its turn described at the time and as follows:

There comes a great white angel of the heights shining with the light of sunshine upon snow. On every side his far-flung aura gleams with brilliant hues, ordered in successive bands from central form to aura's edge, pale rose, pale blue, soft green and purple.   From his head a widening stream of white and fiery force arises and from behind the form flow waves of power suggesting auric wings.

The face is strong, virile, masculine.   The brow is broad, the eyes wide apart and alight with power.   The "hair" is formed of flashes of flame, like fiery power shooting upwards from the head.   The nose and chin are delicately yet strongly modelled, the lips full, the whole face instinct with the majesty and power of the mountain range.   The form itself is veiled by streams of white, flowing energy.   At intervals, throughout the form and outward-flowing power there flashes a white radiance, dazzlingly bright, as of the sunlit snows.

He answers my call for light, "speaking" as if in a deep, resonant bass,[1] vibrant as if with the power of the Earth itself:

"The Gods await the conscious reunion of the mind of man with the Universal Mind.   Humanity awakens slowly. Matter-blinded through centuries, few men as yet perceive the Mind within the substance, the Life within the form.

"In search of power and wealth, men have traversed the whole Earth, have penetrated the wilds, scaled the peaks and conquered the polar wastes.   Let them now seek within the form, scale the height of their own consciousness, penetrate its depths, in search of that inner Power and Life by which alone they may become strong in will and spiritually enriched.

"He who thus throws open his life and mind to the Universal Life and Mind indwelling in all things, will enter into union therewith and to him the Gods will appear.

---

[1] Though such communication is purely mental, words, and even an impression of vocal timbre, are sometimes conveyed to the brain.

"Let him with full intent of mind and will thus meditate:

'Power universal,
Life indwelling,
Mind all-pervading,
I am one with Thee.

'Gods of Power, Life and Mind,
I greet you.
In the Self of the Universe, we are one.
I am that Self, that Self am I.' "

CHAPTER II

THE EARTH'S ANGELIC HIERARCHIES

ONE STUPENDOUS WHOLE

OCCULT science affirms that the universe, as spirit and matter, life and form, consciousness and vehicles, with all its constituents and inhabitants, is a single organism, a living unity. All individuals are as centres, organs or cells in a higher Being, of whom they are a manifestation and a part. These higher Beings in their turn are expressions of the power, the life and the consciousness of still more highly evolved Intelligences. This hierarchical system culminates in one all-inclusive All-Being, the summation and synthesis of all creation, the supreme Deity, the One Alone.

As all the atoms, cells and organs of the human body are unified in that organism, so all beings are unified within the one all-embracing divine Power, Life and Consciousness and its various vehicles, from the most tenuous to the most dense. Those vehicles in their turn constitute the visible and invisible universe which is created by the One Power, sustained by the One Life, shaped, directed and transformed by the One Intelligence, ordered by One Law and composed, fundamentally, of One Element.

Physically, the universe displays exuberant variety and richness of individuality of apparently separate beings and forms. Superphysically, however, the unifying, vital principle begins to be perceived. Spiritually, all is seen to be the product and expression of one deific, creative Power under the operation of one immutable Law.

THE SCREEN OF TIME AND SPACE

An analogy may perhaps be taken from the cinema. Numerous continually-moving forms appear on the screen. If the beam between the projector and the screen be observed, especially if the picture be coloured, only the changes in colour, light and shade can be perceived. These changes, in their turn, are produced by the passage in front of the source of light of the film on which the original pictures were taken. This film itself, though invisible to the audience, is the factor which determines the nature of the phenomena appearing on the screen. The figures on the screen, the changes and the movements in the beam and the pictures on the film strip are all numerous and diverse. Behind them all, however, is the single light by which the pictures themselves are produced, and without which they could not be made to appear.

If the analogy—admittedly not quite perfect—be applied to the phenomena revealed to man through his senses, the space-time universe corresponds to the screen. The beam represents creative energy emitted from its Source, passing through the superphysical worlds to produce the visible universe. The lens represents Creative Mind, through which Archetypes are focussed on to the universal screen. The film corresponds to the archetypal "forms" and the single light represents the primary effect of the activity of the One Creative Power (the current) by which all things were made. Just as the figures on the screen, the beam, the lens, the rolls of film, the light and electrical current, are all part of one co-ordinated scheme for the projection of pictures, so all the apparently separated portions of the universe are, in reality, parts of a single mechanism. The function of this animate "machine" charged with life-force is to create, project into matter and ultimately perfect myriads of previously-conceived substances, objects and beings.

SOLAR ARCHANGELS

This principle of unity amidst diversity is well exemplified by the Kingdom of the Gods. The totality of the Angelic Hosts and nature spirits of a Solar System is a manifestation of one Solar Archangel of unimaginable splendour, within whom all angels live, move and have their being. From this centre and source of their existence all have emanated, and into it all will ultimately return.

In order to manifest, the One Supreme Being becomes expressed in three modes of activity, Three Aspects, each of which may be presumed to find expression as an archangel only slightly less great than the One Alone. These Three are creative, preserving and transforming Aspects, masculine, androgyne and feminine creative potencies, and in their representative and presiding Archangels one of those forces will predominate. Although three mighty Beings, they are also projections and expressions of the Primordial One. These three Emanations in their turn unite in every possible combination to produce a sevenfold self-expression of the Divine Monad. Each such expression is represented in the Angelic Kingdom by a lofty Archangel, and all these together are referred to in Christianity as the Seven Mighty Spirits before the Throne, and elsewhere as the Seven Archangels of the Face, the Cosmocratores, the Sephiroth.

The creative impulse shines forth as light from the One, through the Three and the Seven to produce, at the highest spiritual levels and under the laws of number and harmony, the ideal forms, the Archetypes of every living thing in all kingdoms of Nature, including the human and the angelic. An Archangel presides over each stage of the projection of the Archetype. At every degree of densification, in each successively denser plane of Nature, angels of appropriate Orders embody the power and intent of the Creative Will-Thought and assist in its expression as evolving forms. This hierarchical system obtains throughout all levels, each of the lower groups being an expression of a single higher Intelligence.

On the astral and etheric planes,[1] non-individualised nature spirits are the lowest Order in the hierarchy of the Angelic Hosts. In their purely instinctive response to the will-thought of their seniors, and in their apparently aimless, though unconsciously purposeful, play, they correspond somewhat to the various shades and colours moving in the beam of the cinema projector, the visible universe coming into existence as the result of their creative activity.

This hierarchical method of self-expression by the primordial, deific Principle, is also in operation through Orders of angelic directors of the evolution of life and form in areas of differing dimensions. A single Archangel thus presides over the Solar System as a whole. Each of its major parts is also under the direction of an Intelligence of appropriate evolutionary stature. Our Earth, for example, as a physical unit composed of earth, water, air, fire and ether and its superphysical planes and life, is a vehicle for the Archangel of the planet. For this Being, each of the physical and superphysical planes or spheres—seven in all—which together constitute the whole Earth, is a vehicle of consciousness. The vast company of Solar and Planetary angelic beings is sometimes referred to as the Army of the Light and the Hosts of the Logos.

[1] The universe consists of seven worlds or planes, each composed of matter of seven degrees of density; the physical and etheric combine to form the densest, followed in order by the astral, mental, intuitional, spiritual and two others as yet beyond the range of human consciousness. Vide *An Outline of Theosophy*, C. W. Leadbeater, and *First Principles of Theosophy*, C. Jinarājadāsa, T. P. H., Adyar.

PLANETARY ARCHANGELS

The Archangels or Spiritual Regents of the planets, each of whom maintains an Ambassador and an "Embassy" on Earth, have been referred to somewhat graphically as Heavenly Snails [1] who move with apparent slowness on their orbits round the sun, each carrying their physical planet on their back like a house or shell. The astrological attributes and psychological, mental and spiritual influences of heavenly bodies emanate in large measure from these ensouling Intelligences.

The Archangel of a planet may be regarded as a synthesis of all other Archangels, angels and nature spirits within the planetary field. Immediately below the planetary Archangel may perhaps be placed the Archangels of each of the seven planes or spheres, all the substance of each of which is a vehicle for the Archangel of that plane. From this it follows that each of the apparently individual angels of a plane is, in reality, an expression of the power, the life and the consciousness of that plane as a whole and of its Archangel. Comprehension of this fundamental unity is all important in achieving contact, communion and collaboration with the greater and lesser Gods.

Magic, it is said, is the process of producing visible, physical results determined upon by the trained will-thought of the magician who has found the way to communicate with the appropriate angelic Intelligences and win their collaboration. Magic has therefore been described as the power to address the Gods in their own tongues.

THE CHERUBIM

The One Law also finds expression in great Archangels of Light and is administered by them. These are said to be four in number, each with innumerable subordinates in

[1] Vide *The Secret Doctrine*, H. P. Blavatsky, Vol. I, p. 164 and IV, p. 269, Adyar Edition.

hierarchical order fulfilling the Law according to the twofold
principle of equilibrium and cause and effect. These Four
are sometimes called the *Lipika*,[1] or Recorders, and sometimes
the *Devarajas* of the four quarters of the compass, the Rulers
of the North, the South, the East and the West. They are
personified in the Egyptian religion by the great law-giver
and chronologer, Tehuti and the four Sons of Horus, Mestha,
Hapi, Tuamutef and Qebhsennuf; in Judaism [2] by the Four
Holy Living Creatures, the Cherubim, or sometimes as a single
Cherub with four faces—of a man, an eagle, a lion and an
ox—and by various three or four-headed beings in other
systems of angelology. In Christianity the *Lipika*—assigned
to the Order of angels known as the Watchers—are personified as the Recording Angel who writes in a great book men's
deeds by which they are judged.

THE FIERY CROSS

The idea is not easy to comprehend that different kinds
of energy, each with its own occult properties, flow to and
from the four directions of space and that an Archangel is
stationed at each quarter as Director of that energy. In
further explanation it may therefore be said that the Creative
Fire is conceived as descending vertically from zenith to nadir
to penetrate hitherto virginal, pre-cosmic substance or space,
regarded diagrammatically as horizontal. A cross is thus
formed, the point of penetration being at the intersection of
the arms. This point in space denotes the centre from which
the creative and constructive process arises to transform chaos
into Cosmos. Here is the central sun. Here, the Logos as
Creative Intelligence and Power establishes the Cosmic
Archetype or Ideation from which all develops under the
rule of Time, or throughout successive cycles.

[1] Lofty Intelligences who, as Officials of the Inner Government of the Solar System,
administer the *karmic* law. The Lords of *Karma*.
[2] *Ezekiel*, I, 5, 6.

The thought-imbued, descending Creative Fire radiates horizontally from the point of intersection chiefly in the four lateral directions or to the North, the South, the East and the West, to which it is self-limited for purposes of manifestation. With the existing vertical rays, the six-armed cross is thus formed, which is the fiery core of the resultant Cosmos. The Cosmic Christos is symbolically crucified upon this cross and this is mirrored in the Crucifixion of the historical Christ.

Each of the six creative rays or six arms of the cross is conceived as possessing distinctive characteristics which find expression in an Order of Intelligences. Thus to each quarter is attributed a special influence and an Archangel with its associated Angelic Hosts, one hierarchy being stationed at each corner of the Universe, as it were. Each Archangel is also a Lord of one of the four elements, the fifth, aether, being associated with the centre of the cross. As previously stated, these Intelligences are the Sacred Four of World Religions, the Mind-born Sons of *Brahma* and the Four *Devarajas* of Hinduism, the Cherubim and the four-faced Archangels of Kabbalism and Judaism, including the four symbolic animals of the vision of Ezekiel and associated with the four Evangelists.

The cosmic, fiery cross is said to revolve round its vertical axis, as does the physical Cosmos round its Central Sun. This gyratory motion is reproduced throughout Nature as the axial revolutions of suns, planets and spinning chemical atoms in which electrons and other particles follow planetary paths round their nuclei. Solar Systems, both in groups and individually, and their component planets, also move through space on orbital paths round central suns.

These axial and orbital motions of stellar, solar, planetary and atomic bodies are physical manifestations of the revolutions round the central Spiritual Sun at the nave or hub, of the six-armed cosmic, fiery cross of three dimensions of which the swastika is a two-dimensional symbol. The swastika is an equal-armed cross with short secondary arms at right angles to the primary ones. These hooks, as they are sometimes called, represent the flames and sparks which stream backwards as the fiery, *fohatic* [1] cross revolves continuously throughout creative Day.

Vortices, cosmic, nebular, stellar, solar, planetary and atomic, whirlwinds in space, maelstroms in matter—and perhaps the *chakras* of animals and men—are produced by this vast circumgyration of the cosmic cross of Creative Fire. "*Fohat*," it is said, "digs through space seven holes." [2] *Fohat*, however, is not electrical energy alone. It is endowed with intelligence. It is, in fact, a Being, though inconceivable as such by man, an Archangel of Fire, a veritable God. The vertical descent of fiery power, of horizontal radiations into the four quarters of the spherical field, the revolution of the resultant cross, the formation of vortical centres at the heart and along the arms and the creation and densification of universes and their components according to cruciform and vortical designs—all this is directed by the so-called Seven Sons (and Brothers) of *Fohat*, the great Gods of the six directions of space, the Cosmocratores, the Archangels of the Face, the Sephiroth.

THE COSMIC CRUCIFIXION

The Seventh, the synthesis, the Cosmic Logos, the Spiritual Sun, the Christos by whom all things were made, is enthroned at the centre. Thereon, throughout *Manvantara*, He is voluntarily self-crucified, not in agony and death and downflowing sweat and blood, but in creative ecstasy and with perpetually outpoured power and life. The Mighty Four, the Cherubim, who are also the Recorders of the activities

---

[1] *Fohat*, Tibetan. The constructive Force of Cosmic Electricity polarised into positive and negative electricity.

[2] Vide *The Secret Doctrine*, H. P. Blavatsky, Vol. I, p. 203, Adyar Edition.

of the successive Nights and Days down to the minutest events occurring to the smallest lives, the *Lipika* or Archangels of Time and Law, are stationed at the extremities of the horizontal arms. These four cosmic Beings at the arms of the horizontal cross are the master-mathematicians, as it were, who comprehend the inconceivable complexity of the everchanging-and ever-growing network of the *karmas* [1] of all universes, planets and beings. Since representatives of these Angels of *karma* administer the *karmic* law on this planet in order to effect the greatest possible evolutionary advancement and the strictest justice for every individual, they and their planetary agents, the *karmadevas*, must be included amongst the Angelic Hierarchies of our Earth.

NATIONAL ANGELS [2]

The whole human race is presided over by a lofty Archangel who exerts continually a spiritualising influence upon the Higher Selves of all men. This Archangel of the human race unifies itself at the level of Spiritual Will, or Atma with every human Ego, and by lending its own far more highly developed Atmic power to each, enhances for them the influence of their own Monad and its Ray. The degree of such enhancement and man's response thereto varies through thousands of centuries according to the effect of cyclic progression and the culmination and coincidence of component cycles. Nevertheless it is to be assumed that this ministration continues without intermission throughout the whole world period [3] the duration of which, in terms of physical time, has been said to be at least fifty million years.

[1] See footnote, 2, p. 42.

[2] Part of the subject matter under this heading appeared in my book, *The Coming of the Angels*, now out of print, published by Rider & Co.. by whose kind permission it is included in a revised form in this work.

[3] The time during which the seven Races of men in succession occupy a planet in one Round. Vide *The Solar System*, A. E. Powell, T. P. H., London.

Each well-established nation is similarly presided over by a National Angel or Archangèl Potentate. This lofty Intelligence is associated more especially with the Egos of all members of the nation. It unifies itself with each and continually enhances the spiritual power and life of the Ego. On occasion it also sends an impulse down to the personality to act in a manner which will best contribute to the fulfilment of *dharma* [1] and evolution to the stature of the perfect man.

A National Angel may be studied from two distinct points of view. According to one aspect, he may be regarded as a member of the more elevated ranks of the Angelic Hierarchy who has been appointed to this high office. In that capacity he works largely from the level of Spiritual Will, from which he obtains a full knowledge of the *karma* [2] and the *dharma* of his nation, and of the ideal development towards which it is part of his duty to guide and inspire its people. His work is to quicken the evolution of his nation and to inspire its leaders to make decisions which will help towards the fulfilment of the national *dharma*; he seeks to minimise the effects of errors and to exercise a restraining influence, so that the nation may not depart unduly from the path leading to its highest destiny, or fail to take its appointed place in the family of nations.

As previously stated, above the National Angels of the world there is a still greater Being, who serves the whole human race on this planet in a manner similar to that in which the National Angel serves his particular race. Superior to this Official there are, in all probability, interplanetary Angels who serve the whole of humanity in one Planetary Round, Chain and Scheme. [3] No doubt this hierarchical

[1] *Dharma*, Sanskrit. Duty, task, destiny, right fulfilment, general contribution to and place in the scheme of life.

[2] See footnote 2, p. 42. The adverse or favourable reaction resulting from conduct, *e.g.*, ill-treatment of indigent populations of colonised countries produces adverse *karma*, whilst help rendered to necessitous peoples generates favourable *karma*. Since both are educative, all *karma* is ultimately beneficent.

[3] In occult science, the Solar System is said to consist of ten Planetary Schemes, each composed of seven successive Chains of globes, superphysical and physical. Each Chain is

system is extended to include Solar Systems, and even Cosmoi, all of which are linked together by angelic beings of increasing spiritual stature.

A somewhat similar hierarchical method would seem to be employed by the advanced members of the human race forming the Great White Brotherhood of Adepts,[1] who guide and guard humanity throughout the ages. There are Adepts responsible for the evolution of individual nations, still higher Officials who have charge of continents, and above them the great Planetary Adept, Ruler, the Spiritual King who is the earthly Representative of the Solar Logos. Complete and perfect co-operation is maintained between the human and angelic branches of this Inner Government of the World. In the future, as higher orders of consciousness are unfolded and a wider range of sensory response is developed, the human ministers responsible for the religious, governmental and cultural development of a nation will doubtless consciously collaborate with their spiritual superiors in both human and angelic hierarchies. Then, at last, this earth will enter upon the longed-for Golden Age.

To return to the conditions of the present time, the international Race Angel may be thought of as a weaver who uses as his threads the national characteristics, the *dharma* and the *karma* of the nations of the world, weaving them as the centuries pass into the pattern which the nations will produce according to the plan held in the Universal Mind, "the pattern on the mount". By his weaving he is also drawing the races together, helping to establish on earth the brotherhood of man. In spite of his mighty power and his perfect understanding of the divine Plan, he seeks neither to impose his

---

composed of seven Rounds, during each of which the life-stream, bearing with it the evolving beings, travels once round the seven globes. The period of occupation of one of the seven globes is called a world period. Vide *The Solar System*, A. E. Powell.

[1] Vide *The Masters and the Path*, C. W. Leadbeater, T. P. H., Adyar.

will upon men nor to oppose the collective will of a nation, however wrongly that will may be directed at any particular period. For man must grow by virtue of his own experience and the unfolding life within him.

The other aspect from which the National Angel may be studied is more difficult to understand and to explain, for it pertains to abstract levels of consciousness. In addition to the Angel's life and work as an individual, he is also the summation of the whole national consciousness. The millions of Egos incarnated in a nation to form the national Oversoul are united in him. The three aspects of a nation's life, the national *karma*, *dharma* and consciousness, meet and find a single expression in the National Angel.

Under the Lords of *Karma*, the National Angel is granted a certain amount of latitude and control in the working out of the nation's *karma*. He can concentrate it, so that sections are paid off quickly or he can extend it over long periods. He has a complete knowledge of his nation's capacity to endure adversity, of the amount of adverse *karma* it is capable of bearing without suffering serious evolutionary delay. He is also able to balance the favourable against the adverse *karma* of the nation, to modify present conditions by drawing on *karma* from the past.

In all this ministration, the Angel looks to the future and to the fulfilment of the national *dharma*. He not only lends his own power, but also utilises the capacities and characteristics of the nation in guiding it towards the fulfilment of its highest destiny. In the realm of Egoic consciousness, he is able at a given period to accentuate national traits so that the nation, if responsive, then tends to pursue a particular course. If the forces and qualities of a people are thought of as being visible in terms of colour, then he may be said to cause a special colour or group of colours to shine out at certain times with greater luminosity in the consciousness of the nation.

Such, in small part, is the nature and the activity of an Angel-Ruler. Occult tradition assigns to the Goddess, Pallas Athene, at least down to the end of the Golden Age, the office of Archangelic Ruler of the Grecian nation.

ANGEL BUILDERS OF HUMAN FORMS

Every human individual is also on occasion under the direct care of a member of one of the Orders of the Angelic Hosts. Each cycle of human rebirth is presided over by members of the Orders of angels which are especially associated with man. As stated in Part I, Chapter IV, at each successive rebirth individual human Egos receive the special assistance of angels responsible for the construction of mental, emotional, etheric and physical forms. These angels operate partly under the direction of representatives of the *Lipika*. The choice of era, continent, nation, religion, parents, environment and opportunity, sex, type and condition of body and degree of potential or actual health and disease, are all decided according to Law by these presiding Intelligences and corresponding Adept officials. The several *karmas* of the incarnating Ego, of the natal nation, of members of groups with whom there will be association, of the whole family and of the future husband or wife and children, are all fully considered. The inherent rhythm of the Monad-Ego, the ultimate destiny according to Monadic temperament or Ray, the past *karma* and the immediate and future missions are all reviewed and with unfailing justice the most favourable choices are made under *karmic* circumstances.

Since the number of Monads using the Earth as a planetary field is stated to be sixty thousand million, and all of those who are at present passing through the human kingdom receive this ministration, angels of the Order responsible for the descent of the human Ego into incarnation are thus included in this enumeration of the angelic population of our globe.

The function of these beings is partially described in the above-mentioned Chapter.

ANGELS OF RELIGIONS

Each major World Religion has its Archangel and angelic ministrants appointed by high planetary Officials, Adèpt and Archangelic. The highest of the Archangels of Religions preside over the reservoirs of spiritual power appointed to each World Faith. They conserve and supply this power as it is invoked, to the end of the maximum effectiveness. Each duly consecrated Temple, Mosque, Cathedral, Abbey, Church and Oratory is placed under the direction of a presiding angel of the Order associated with World Religions. These conserve both the power apportioned to the particular edifice and that which is generated at the ceremony of Consecration. They also receive and direct the uprising streams of human aspiration, worship and prayer and the power, force and devotion evoked by ceremonial. In addition, they transmit the responses from the Deity, the World Teacher, the Angelic Hosts and Members of the Communion of Saints, together with the descending power from the reservoir.

The supreme Teacher of Angels and of Men, known in the East as the *Bodhisattva* and in the West as the Lord Christ, has under His direction, it is said, great companies of Archangels and angels, who find in His service their continual delight. In His perpetual ministration to all mankind and to the members of the angelic and sub-human kingdoms, He sends out according to their needs great streams of power, wisdom, blessing, inspiration, healing and love. He employs hosts of angels to conserve, direct and apply these expressions of His loving compassion for all that lives.

Angels also attend religious services for purposes of devotion, and certain of them may be seen reverently hovering within the radiance which surrounds the consecrated Elements.

The Eucharistic Ceremony is under the direction of an exalted Angel, sometimes called the Angel of the Eucharist. At the moment of the Consecration of the Elements, a glorious Angelic Being in the likeness of the Lord Christ, known as the Angel of the Presence, descends upon the Altar as His angelic representative. At the chanting of the Preface, when reference is made to the Nine Orders of the Angels recognised in Christian angelology, who are none other than the Sephirothal Angels, a representative of each Order responds to the Invocation and bestows the power, light and benediction of his Order upon Officiants, congregation, Church and surrounding regions.[1]

Other World Religions have equally the assistance of appointed Orders of the Angelic Hosts. The great Hindu *mantric* [2] ceremony, known as the *Gayatri*, calls down Solar power and is the occasion for ministration to mankind by Archangels and angels especially associated with the sun.[3]

All other valid (occultly effective and accepted by Adept and Archangel Officials) ceremonial Orders throughout the world, and especially those which, like Freemasonry, originated in the Lesser and Greater Mysteries and are still representative of them, also receive the benediction, the presence and the co-operation of angels and Archangels.

GROUP SOUL ANGELS

The evolving, conscious life of the animal, plant, mineral and elemental kingdoms of Nature, as previously stated, is under the direction of appropriate Orders of angels. This life is not individualised, as is the case in the human kingdom,

---

[1] For a fuller description of the ministry of the angels in the Christian Church, see *The Science of the Sacraments* C. W. Leadbeater, and *The Inner Side of Church Worship*, Geoffrey Hodson,

[2] *Mantra*, Sanskrit. A rhythmic arrangement of sounds, generally Sanskrit syllables, which when correctly intoned generate and release potent energies, *e.g.*, the Sacred Syllable *OM* and the mystic sentence: *Om mani padme hum*, Amen, *Kyrie Eleison*, and some Greek and Latin words and sentences.

[3] Vide *The Lotus Fire*, G. S. Arundale, T. P. H., Adyar.

where each human being is a fully self-conscious, responsible individual.[1]   Vast areas of the Earth with its mineral contents, large numbers of trees, plants and insects, and smaller numbers of animals and birds, are physical vehicles for a specific, ensouling life which is called a Group, Soul.   The evolution of Group Souls reaches its apotheosis in the animal kingdom, in which the number of physical representatives becomes smaller and smaller until at last the process of individualisation—generally of a domestic animal—occurs and a human soul is born.   This aeonic unfoldment and development is continuously supervised and aided by angelic ministrants, amongst whom are those who direct the process of the division of the animal Group Soul into single human entities.[2]

THE INSECT KINGDOM

An Angelic Order exists which has evolved through the insect-branch of Nature.   Universal Mind contains the ideation of all possible modes and forms of manifestation.   The primordial ideation and Archetype includes the insect kingdom in all its immense variety.   Monads evolve through that kingdom ultimately to become Solar and Cosmic Archangels associated, though not exclusively with, that creative Ray.

If, in view of the fact that certain insects are inimical to man, this concept should appear strange, it must be remembered that parasitism, for example, is only loathsome when the host is conscious of disequilibrium set up by the parasite. The types most objectionable in man's eyes, the disease-carrying and the blood-sucking, are no more repulsive in reality than any other parasite.   Since parasitism is the principle by which physical life is enabled to persist, logically no individual parasite can be condemned, however much its depredations must be resisted.   The inherent divinity of the more

[1] Vide *A Study in Consciousness*, A. Besant, T. P. H., Adyar.
[2] Vide *The Causal Body*, A. E. Powell, T. P. H., London.

harmless and beautiful members of the insect kingdom is easier to recognise than that of those which appear ugly and are hurtful to man. To many minds, the beauty of the dragon-fly, the moth and the butterfly, would be their justification.

Just as Monads, manifested through other facets of divine ideation, are guarded and aided by their evolutionary seniors, so are those who, when their Rays first touch the physical world, find their embodiment as thousands of tiny insects. From then on throughout their upward journey, which will culminate in becoming a perfected, divine being on one of the Seven Rays [1] into which, the insect kingdom, like every other, is classifiable, they are the subject of ministration by their seniors. They pass their physical existence and achieve all that is desired of them by passage through that kingdom as butterflies, bees, beetles, ants or other leading examples of the insect Ray types, and pass on to the superphysical worlds through which first as nature spirits and later as *rupa* [2] and *arupa devas*, they ascend to Archangelic heights and beyond. Monads passing through the insect kingdom and the forms which they ensoul are therefore of equal importance with all other manifestations, facets, modes and forms of divine existence. Presiding over their Rays, their Orders and their species are Archangels and angels, who not only shepherd the indwelling life but preserve and fashion to greater beauty the insect form. Their presence as guardians and tutors stimulates into action the natural instinct of the numerous species to pursue those physical habits by which the genus is perpetuated, the stages of gestation are successfully passed through, food is found, mating is performed and eggs are deposited.

[1] See footnote 1, p. 42.
[2] *Rupa, arupa,* Sanskrit. Form and formless, referring to the levels respectively below and above the fourth subplane of the mental plane. In the former, the tendency to assume shape preponderates over rhythm and in the latter rhythm or the free flow of life predominates. Angels of the *rupa* planes present more definitely to human consciousness the idea of bodily form than do those of *arupa* levels.

The mass instinct or race memory which leads each variety to pursue its appropriate modes of life is stimulated and directed by the angel tutors of the insect kingdom of Nature. In some cases, in earlier *Manvantaras* they themselves have evolved through that kingdom and know well its ways and needs. Such angels would be embodiments, however tenuous their forms, of that aspect of the One Mind which finds expression and expansion in and through the insect world. The all-protective, maternal Mind cares for its progeny in every realm, partly by enclosing it within its protective and guiding thought and partly by the ministrations of certain Orders of the Angelic Hosts. The Group Souls of insects, as also of birds, which find embodiment in very large numbers of forms, are all under the direction of senior angel officials, each supported or assisted by junior members of its own Order. Under this protection and tuition the whole insect kingdom, like every other, evolves to higher states, to more beautiful forms and to increased intelligence.

The development to which this process leads in Rounds and Chains which follow the present Fourth (of each) can only be assumed. There is, for example, a possibility. supported by hints in occult literature, that so high a degree of development of insect mind and form could be reached that individualisation could occur and further evolution be continued in that form. This obtains in the present ascent from the human to the superhuman kingdoms when the same physical form is used, if one is retained, or the same kind of form is assumed, if a new one is taken. Admittedly, the idea of an insect, butterfly, ant, bee or beetle as large or as intelligent as modern man might regard himself to be, may at first seem fantastic. If, however, one grants the prolonged continuance of the evolutionary processes observable throughout Nature and the existence and action of both Universal Mind and its angelic embodiments, then there is at least nothing illogical in the supposition.

Beelzebub, the so-called, if mis-called, God of Flies [1] may perhaps be regarded as an enemy of a human race which suffers from certain classes of insects, but if thought of as a Lord of Scarabs [2] or, indeed, of all insect life, Beelzebub, thus conceived, is divine rather than Satanic. It is sometimes necessary to divest oneself of certain preconceptions in order to be receptive to truth. This applies especially to the popular ideas of such postulations as Satan, Moloch and Beelzebub as Directors of processes and Lords of creatures which appear evil to man; for the involutionary procedure which such imaginary beings partly personify is as important as the evolutionary process for which it is a preparation. Bees gather honey and so feed man; they pollinate flowers and in this way also feed man. Bees sting in self-protection and their sting is painful and can be mortal to man, but they should not therefore be regarded as evil in themselves.

A DEVA OF THE BEE KINGDOM [3]

My own observations have led me to a belief in the existence of protective and directive angel guardians of bees. Once, whilst watching some hives, I became aware of a very lofty angel established at the level of abstract thought, whose aura displayed the typical colours of the bee body sublimated to the higher mental level of intensity and delicacy of light and colour. This Intelligence appeared to be an agent of an Archangel presiding over the whole of bee life, consciousness, form and evolution upon this planet. My notes made at the time state that a hierarchy of angels serves under this

[1] Vide Part III, Chapter V, "Inverse Sephiras and the Problem of Evil".
[2] A kabbalistic concept.
[3] Part of the subject matter under this heading appeared in my book, *The Coming of the Angels*, now out of print, published by Rider & Co., by whose kind permission it is included in a revised form in this work.

Archangel and is represented at the etheric level by the nature
spirit builders of the physical forms of bees.   There was such
an angel connected with the hives at which this study was
made, and presumably there would be one with every active
hive.   These angels closely resemble other angels associated
with the subhuman kingdoms of Nature in temperament and
appearance, but yellow, gold and dark browns predominate
in their auras.   They seem to regard the evolution of the bee
as of very great importance and to take seriously, though
joyously, their work of directing, guarding and quickening
the evolution of bee consciousness.   They are in continuous
contact with their superiors and, through them, with the planetary Archangel or Overlord of bees.

The queen bee in a hive shows astrally as a golden centre
of glowing light and colour within the luminous aura of the
hive.   She shines therein as a nucleus, and is a centre of life,
superphysically as well as physically.   Forces are continually
flowing through her into the hive group soul; these consist
of life-forces and certain electro-magnetic, creative energies
for which she is a centre or focus in the hive.   These forces
flow outwards from the centre in minute ripples and this
ceaseless movement produces a superphysical sound not unlike that of the buzzing of the bees.   The shape of the aura
of the hive and community is that of the old-fashioned straw
hive, i.e., a pointed dome with a flat base.   Each bee appears
to superphysical vision as a speck or point of light, the queen's
aura being larger and brighter than that of the other bees.

The angel appears to work especially for those of his
charges who are at the larva phase and to exercise a very distinct and definite protecting and guiding function at that
stage, almost as though bees on this planet were not yet quite
capable, without such help, of passing through all the growth
processes after hatching.   The angel also influences the selec-
tion, special feeding and development of the queen and makes

the necessary links between the permanent atoms,[1] the bee
over-soul and the selected queen.

The consciousness of the bee is instinctive and the many
evidences of ordered community life amongst bees result
from a high development of that instinct, rather than of intelligence. Here, again, the work of the angel is of considerable
importance in awakening the instincts of the different groups
in the community and in arousing the impulse towards certain
courses of conduct. Broadly, one might say that the queen
is the life centre of the community and the angel the directing
intelligence. He unifies his mind with the group consciousness of the hive and is to some extent imprisoned therein,
submitting to that limitation for the sake of the service it
enables him to render. Outside the hive, however, he has a
certain measure of freedom of consciousness though at the
emotional and mental levels he seems permanently attached
to it, as if his complete withdrawal would mean an absence
of control, and consequent disorder in the community. Under
this limitation there is no sense of restriction; on the contrary,
there is an absorbing interest and delight in the work, the joy
of the craftsman and the artist. The angel is responsible for
the development of both life and form, and is happy in the
knowledge that he is helping to perfect these and is playing
his part in the great evolutionary plan. Just as plants and
trees are developing emotion, the bee is developing mind.
The queen represents the nascent higher, abstract mind, the
workers the lower, concrete mind, the drones the creative
principle. The creative urge is experienced as instinct, rather
than desire; feeling exists, but is reduced to a minimum, as
if it had long ago been sublimated.

The angel, from whom I sought counsel, indicated that
attempts by man to co-operate with his kingdom were wel-
comed and expressed the hope that they foreshadowed the

[1] Vide *A Study in Consciousness*, A. Besant, T. P. H., Adyar.

approach of an era of human and angelic co-operation in bee culture, as well as in other branches of husbandry. Bees will respond, he said to attempts by man to unify his consciousness with theirs, just as plants respond, however faintly, to admiration and affection. But there is a distinct danger of over-development in the culture of bees. Their organisation is marvellously adaptable, but if they are over-exploited, and if the hives are made too complex and artificial, harm will be done. Man must recognise the evolving life in the bee, and not regard that insect as a mere mechanical honey-gatherer for the sole benefit of the human race.

In other fields, other Orders of angels and nature spirits perform analogous functions and use the Earth as a field of evolution and activity, references being made to some of them in later parts of this work. Numerous other Orders of angels are using this Earth as a field of evolution and activity. Information concerning them is contained in Hindu and Buddhist Scriptures, the literature of Kabbalism and in that great synthesis of Occult Science, *The Secret Doctrine*, by H. P. Blavatsky.

CHAPTER III

THE COLOUR LANGUAGE OF THE ANGELS [1]

A NGELIC forms are built of light, or rather of tenuous material which is self-luminous; for every atom of their bodies, as also of the worlds in which they dwell, is a glowing particle of light. The form they use closely resembles our own and is, in fact, built upon the same model as is the human physical body. As stated earlier and shown in the illustrations, fairies and angels thus generally appear as very beautiful, ethereal human-like beings. Their faces, however, wear an expression which is distinctly non-human, for they are stamped with an impression of dynamic energy, of vividness of consciousness and life, with a certain supernal beauty and an other-worldliness which is rarely seen among men.

The appearance of the angels is also remarkable to human sight on account of the continual play of energy within and through their bodies and their glowing auras. They may be thought of both as agents, and even engineers, of the fundamental forces of Nature. The powers which they control and manipulate are continually passing through and radiating from them, producing as they flow an effect which somewhat resembles the aurora.

Distinct force-centres, vortices and certain clearly defined lines of force are visible in their bodies. In the auric

---

[1] Part of the subject matter under this heading appeared in my book, *The Coming of the Angels*, now out of print, published by Rider & Co., by whose kind permission it is included in a revised form in this work.

discharges definite forms are produced, which sometimes suggest a crown upon the head and outspread wings of brilliant and ever-changing hues. The auric pinions, however, are not used for flying, for angels move swiftly through the air at will, with a graceful, floating motion and need no aids to flight. The old painters and writers, some of whom seem to have caught glimpses of them, apparently mistook these flowing forces for their clothing and their wings, and so depicted them as robed in human dress, and even gave the angels feathers in their wings.

As their bodies are formed of light, every variation in the flow of force produces a change of colour. A change of consciousness is instantly visible as an alteration in the shape and colour of their auras. An outpouring of love, for example, suffuses them with a crimson glow while, in addition, a vivid stream of roseate love-force flows out towards the object of their affection. Activity of thought appears as an uprush of yellow light and power from the head, so that they frequently appear as if crowned with a shining halo of light—a crown of gold which is their thought, set with many jewels, each jewel an idea. Perhaps this is the origin of one of their titles in Hinduism, *Chitra Shikhandina*, "the bright-crested".

All the phenomena of emotion and thought which we term subjective, are objective to angels, as also to men endowed with superphysical vision. Angels thus see thought processes, emotions and aspirations as external and material phenomena; for they live in the worlds of feeling, thought, spiritual intuition and spiritual will. Their "speech" produces colour and form rather than sound. A system of symbology is included in their mode of communication, symbols and flashes of colour always appearing in the superphysical worlds as natural expressions of both human and angelic thought. The angels' sense of the oneness of Life is so vivid that their every thought expresses an aspect of the fundamental truth of unity. This gives to their colour conversations a depth and a beauty not present in the ordinary interchange of human thought. They are incapable of a concept either purposeless or untrue, or which fails in some measure to express that inherent divinity of which they never lose consciousness, and which illumines and inspires their every thought and deed. In this respect their colour language somewhat resembles the ancient Senzar, in which each letter and syllable is an expression of a basic truth. Unlike that ancient priestly tongue, however—the product of profoundly inspired minds —the mental language of the angels is instinctive and natural, calling for no conscious effort on their part in the choice and production of colour, form or symbol.

An angel who on occasion has mentally instructed me concerning his [1] Kingdom, also provided examples of angelic communication and of the operation of the law by which superphysical matter assumes appropriate form and colour in response to the impact of thought. An account of two of these lessons is here given from notes taken at the time. I must, however, first explain that *arupa* [2] *devas* are in the highest degree impersonal, impassive, detached. Their consciousness is universal and exclusively concentrated upon their tasks. They are not normally accustomed to experience any personal attachments whatever. *Rupa devas* associated with the evolving life in Nature do not, as far as I am aware, usually experience or express the emotion of personal love. Their minds are universal and their "hearts" belong to the One Life of which they are impersonal embodiments. Certain *rupa devas*, however, may be regarded as incarnations of the qualities of divine love, compassion, tenderness for all that lives and these do feel, in however sublimated and impersonal a manner, a sense of unity with each other and with man.

[1] As before stated, the masculine pronoun is used for convenience only, angels being asexual.

[2] See footnote 2, p. 81.

As the following descriptions indicate, their love power can become temporarily directed to persons but without the faintest tinge of I-ness and possessiveness.

Certain nature spirits on the threshold of individualisation into angelhood, particularly those associated with the element of air—fairies and sylphs—can feel attracted towards men who possess the power consciously to enter their kingdom and communicate with them. Their submission to this attraction is rarely complete and even whilst seeking to allure the object of their affections, they do not usually conceive a permanent relationship. Such close mento-emotional associations with human beings can be helpful to them even though very harmful to their human partner. For them, the attainment of individualisation might be hastened by a blending of their mento-emotional nature with that of an individualised human being, but for man the adventure would be likely to lead to insanity.

Medieval legends in which sylphs and other nature spirits for their own advantage seek, and even physically attain, unions with men are probably more allegorical than historical. Physical union would demand materialisation on the part of the sylph which is most unlikely and, if ever attained, very rare. It would seem to be more probable that a veiled reference is being made to the evolutionary value to such nature spirits of close psychical association and collaboration with members of the human family.

An occult tradition does exist that, as an exception to that impersonality which is characteristic of highly evolved *devas*, intimate egoic attachments with human beings have been formed and have even become so strong as to cause the *deva* to seek and obtain admission to the human kingdom in order to be near the beloved human being. Birth in a human body then follows and, when a physical meeting with the beloved occurs, a very deep and fiery love is awakened in both of them. So strong is this emotion, that, if conventional barriers exist, they are ignored. Tragedy is not infrequently the result.

A CONVERSATION IN COLOUR

Whilst resting in the garden of my cottage in Gloucestershire, I observed the angel teacher travelling at a great height in the air and sent out a greeting and a mental call for further knowledge concerning the Angelic Hosts. At once he paused in his "flight" and descended steeply towards the garden. As he came down, he sent an answering stream of love, which extended from the region of his heart and appeared as rays of glowing rose and crimson light. This outflowing love resembled a flower, for the sides of the funnel form which it produced were divided into petals and in the centre was a brilliant golden "rose", the whole opening gradually as the angel drew near. This "flower" pulsed rhythmically and the lines of force of which it was composed quivered as he poured forth his affection and life-force. He resembled a glorious Greek God, upon whose breast was an open rose. The petal-like radiations reached out and over me, the maximum diameter of the " flower " being about eight feet. A continuous play of brilliantly coloured force in bands of varying size and degrees of luminosity also shone above the angel's head.

Another angel, chiefly blue in colour, soon appeared and the two engaged in "conversation". As they "spoke", their auras reached out towards each other, touched and drew back, like the wings of celestial butterflies. They were about twenty-five yards apart, and a little above the fruit trees in the orchard. The fluidic nature of their auras was demonstrated by the ease with which they extended them to cover the intervening space. They "spoke" both with their hearts and their minds, for colours and symbols appeared in the emotional and mental matter of their auras, above their head for the most part, but also flashing between them with a rapidity and brilliance quite beyond my capacity to observe fully and record accurately. The main theme of the first angel found its natural expression through that soft, pale green sometimes seen in a summer sunset, this shade appearing continually both in the bands of colour above his head and in the symbol formed; it also tinged the larger portion of his aura, suggesting the qualities of sympathy and understanding.

Three beautiful forms like vertical, elongated scallop shells next appeared and hovered in the air above his head, quivering with life and light; in colour they were rose, yellow, and dark blue deepening to purple. Presently they expanded into the shape and appearance of large fans, met and became interwoven into one large, fan-shaped radiation.

A SCALLOP SHELL

tion. Alternately widening and narrowing, the single stream of flowing force extended high into the air and then disappeared. From his brother angel this called forth a perfect blaze of response, like a pyrotechnic display. His first answer turned the upper part of his aura into three bands of colours of the same shades as the shells; it then swept forward and embraced the first angel, holding him thus for some two or three seconds and then withdrawing. Three greatly enlarged fan-shaped symbols next appeared above him in succession, each symbol disappearing into the upper air in a flash of colour. A radiant smile illumined his face, and it was evident that the remark of the first angel had touched some responsive chord in his nature.

The first angel then explained to me the meaning of this interchange. The blue angel who was the second to appear contained within himself something of the fundamental forces and qualities of character underlying the second, fifth and seventh Rays.[1]   His life was an expression of the deepest love and the highest intellect, whilst in his work he displayed perfect precision of action.   These qualities represented his ideal of perfection and he was consciously linked with an Archangel Superior in whom they were fully developed.   In all Nature he perceived predominantly these three powers, traced the effects of their operation in members of the human race and expressed them in all his own activities.

In order to help human beings, for example, he would unify himself with their love nature, enhancing the human power of love by adding to it his own impersonal and universal affection.   He would help scientists by stimulating their mental powers, by increasing their capacity for profound abstraction, and would endeavour to illumine their minds with the solution of any problems which they were seeking to solve. He would assist artists, actors, dancers and ceremonialists to attain greater perfection, grace and beauty of portrayal and more accurate expression of the idea by which their art was inspired.   He would similarly aid his brother angels and the evolving life in the sub-human kingdoms of Nature.   In all his activities these three characteristics would predominate, forming the background of his life and the source of his inspiration.

The first angel, with deep and intuitive sympathy, discerned this fact and mentally expressed his brother angel's ideals with all the fullness and completeness of which he was capable, thereby producing the three shell-like forms in the colours typical of the three Rays. The second angel responded by causing the three highly developed qualities of his nature to shine out successively in greatly enlarged fan-shaped forms.

This account, lengthy as it is, is still but a very incomplete description of an interchange of thought and feeling between

[1] Vide *The Seven Human Temperaments*, Geoffrey Hodson, T.P.H., Adyar.

the angels, which probably lasted no more than a minute. The use of the word "Ray" fails adequately to express the concept in the angel's mind; he would probably call it an aspect of the Divine Life and Consciousness which is projected as a tongue of flame from the central fiery heart of things, or a stream of specially attuned vital energy permeating the universe. These conceptions were included within each of the shell-shaped symbols which, it will be noticed, are apt representations of the fundamental idea. The point of the shell would be at the central source of power which, as it poured forth, would widen out into the fan shape.

Each of these symbols consisted of radiating lines of force, the number of which I was not able to count, though doubtless that also would have its significance. As the whole symbol took form, the lines of force crossed each other and became interwoven until a broad, expanding stream of the three types of energy was formed. Each stream, however, could still be traced, because it maintained its own shape and colour in spite of the interweaving. The combined effect of these three aspects of Life working both in and through the second angel and in Nature was most appropriately portrayed by this shell-like form.

The angel further explained that, in addition to this colour language, there is a direct interchange of ideas at mental levels. The colours and symbols are largely produced by that interchange, though they may also be used as illustrations and elucidations of the central idea.

THE DANCE OF THE SYLPHS

The aerial heights above the district of Gloucestershire in which these teachings were received are peopled with various orders of nature spirits, and especially with sylphs of differing degrees of development. The angel teacher referred to in the preceding description, still remaining near the ground, turned his attention upwards, opened his arms towards the sky and sent out a call which had the effect of bringing a large number of sylphs down into the garden where I was seated. As they descended they drew together in groups, and their blended auras produced the effect of living, sylph-made cloud forms, rose-coloured for the most part and brilliantly self-luminous. They brought with them an atmosphere of superabundant joy, as of a happy band of older children suddenly released from school, though in their case the opposite had occurred, as the angel called them from the freedom of the upper air to serve as subjects for human education.

The summons consisted of a strong and highly concentrated stream of will-power clothed in mental matter, a will-thought, a mental "shout" as it were. From the upper portion of the angel's aura a number of small, cone-shaped forms also flashed into the air point upwards; the main colouring was rose, though the points were tipped with steel-blue. Each one "struck" a sylph, attracted its attention and conveyed an order, in response to which it descended. The angel was so far above them in evolution that an expression of his thought and will amounted to a command.

The angel smiled on them and rose-coloured rays of love shone from the sylphs towards the angel, each one drawing immediate response from him, his aura becoming suffused with a rosy light. He extended it laterally into two wing-like radiations and then stretched these forward until they enveloped and passed beyond the group of sylphs, who were thus played upon by the intensely vivid and luminous auric energies of the angel. With these auric "wings" he maintained a continual, graceful sweeping and swinging movement backwards and forwards between himself and the sylphs, each beat of the "wings" pouring more life and love into them and filling them with an added joy, until their state became one of rapture.

Towards each other, they displayed considerable mutual affection, many of them "standing" with arms outstretched to rest upon each other's shoulders. When these felicitations were completed, a concerted movement began in which all were linked in this way, the whole group arranging itself in circular tiers into the shape of a convolvulus flower. One sylph formed the point; three formed a circle above it, all facing inwards; the remainder formed ring upon ring, each larger than the one below, the whole glowing and flashing with rosy light, within which the natural colours of their auras appeared like the changing hues of an opal. Then the whole "flower" began to turn, all the sylphs moving together and maintaining perfectly the convolvulus flower form. Their faces bore an expression of joy and their long "hair" floated out behind them and their shining auric robes blending in expression of their perfect unity of feeling and of thought.

They revolved with increasing rapidity, until the angel gave the signal of dismissal by his raising his right hand above his head. Then the whole group, still revolving and maintaining the flower formation, rose high into the heavens, after which each ring opened out into a line and broke up into groups of two and three sylphs. Still rotating and rising as it turned, the flower form created in superphysical matter by this aerial dance remained, shining in heavens. Shortly afterwards, as if perceiving this and animated by a new idea, the sylphs re-formed into one big circle round the "flower" and by united thought built an enclosing, translucent sphere of the soft green colour of the teaching angel's aura. This did not "grow" entirely into a closed sphere, but remained open at the top, streams of energy flowing up through the interior of the form to play out into the air above.

A certain abandon now became apparent in the movements of the sylphs, who continued to wheel with extreme rapidity round the flower form. Their heads were thrown back and their bodies were curved outwards from the circle. At last they dispersed glancing and sending towards the angel thoughts of love which descended upon him in a shower of crimson cones. These entered his aura, within which they flowed for a time with rosy light.

The flower form was evidently created as an offering and the dance was an expression of love, unity and joy, performed in honour of the angel who called them, to whom they paid the compliment of building the surrounding form in the predominating colour of his aura. A smile lighted his face as he turned to me in a gesture of farewell, and then disappeared.

CHAPTER IV

THE LESSER GODS

THE ASTRAL AND THE ETHERIC FORMS

O N the lower rungs of the ladder of the Angelic Hierarchy are to be found the nature spirits of the four subtle elements of earth, water, air and fire. The English countryside where these studies were made is well populated with the almost infinite variety of denizens of these four kingdoms of Nature.

My observations suggest that nature spirits use two distinct forms. One of these is the permanent astral body and the other a temporarily materialised etheric vehicle. The astral form consists of a spherical, many-coloured aura surrounding the delicate, force-built fairy form within. The etheric vehicle is assumed for at least two reasons. One is that, when an etheric body is worn, an added sense of individuality or entity is experienced by the nascent mind, which is normally unselfconscious and diffused throughout a group. The other is that an increased vitality and vividness of life are attained by closer contact with the physical world, both during seasons of plant germination, growth and full development, and in bright sunshine. These experiences provide pleasure. Under these conditions nature spirits emerge from the astral into the etheric levels where they become more easily visible and are more generally first seen. There they dance, play, see each other, and human beings to some extent, imitate

them and on occasions become attached to those sufficiently
sensitive to respond to their presence and even communicate
with them.

When the etheric form is assumed, its shape would appear
to be governed by at least three influences. The first of these
is that of the Archetype, which is the same for both the Angelic
and the human kingdoms. The second is the modification
of the Archetype characteristic of the nature spirits of each
of the four elements of earth, water, air and fire. Variations
of each of these are also to be observed at different levels below, on and above the surface of the earth, in diverse natural
conditions and in differing districts.

The third influence is exerted by the human habits, the
dress and the popular thought con-
cerning the appearance of fairy people of particular times and places.
Certain periods in history have thus
left their mark upon the nature spirit
kingdom. The gnome shape apparently dates from the first physical
inhabitants of the planet in ancient
Lemurian [1] days. The impress of
Atlantean thought is still to be seen
upon the Greater and Lesser Gods
of such countries as Central and
South America and the Pacific
Islands and Archipelagos which
were for long periods inhabited by
Atlanteans. The appearance of
other nature spirits of earth is evidently moulded according

GNOME
AFTER PHOTOGRAPH
"IRISH AND THE GNOME"

[1] Lemuria and Atlantis are names given to continents now submerged beneath the
Pacific and Atlantic Oceans respectively. They were the homes of the third and fourth
of the seven major Races of men to occupy this planet. The present Aryan Race and
language group is the fifth of these. The first two Races, being on the downward arc wore
superphysical and etheric bodies only. Vide *The Solar System*, A. E. Powell,
T. P. H., London.

to the medieval European rustic, of whom the brownie is in part a miniature reproduction. Whole tribes of earth nature spirits are to be found in England wearing an Elizabethan style of male attire.[1] Fairies frequently assume a relatively modern appearance, even to the style of "hair," as is also shown in the fairies who were photographed by the two children in Yorkshire.[2] Some nature spirits assume the blacksmith's attire, and even carry thought-made tools, others the cobbler's, whilst others again, consciously or unconsciously, display similar forms of mimicry of human activities, habits and dress.

Fairy thought is powerfully formative upon astral and etheric matter. As far as their limited powers of observation permit, they delight to copy the appearance of such human beings as they can see, an art at which they are very expert. In North America the earth nature spirits are often nude to the waist and wear what appear to be leather or buckskin trousers, these sometimes being fringed after the habit of the American Indian. Their auras, too, are not infrequently arranged in concentric bands of colour, causing them somewhat to suggest the appearance of the Indian war bonnet of dyed eagle feathers. Unclothed, black gnomes resembling aborigines are to be seen in South Africa and Australia whilst certain earth nature spirits in New Zealand look rather like miniature, half-dressed Maori men.

All descriptions of the hair, wings and garments of nature spirits, especially including the appearance of filmy, gossamer-like clothing, refer to densifications, to the level of the fourth sub-plane from above of the ether, of certain inner portions of their astro-etheric auras. Wands, on the other hand, appear spontaneously as symbols of authority, forms naturally assumed by the attribute of rule by instinctual will by

[1] Vide *Fairies*, E. L. Gardner, and especially the photograph of a so-called gnome, a sketch of which appears on the previous page, T. P. H., London.
[2] *Ibid.*

the leaders of concerted movements of nature spirits which control and direct those in their charge.

The consciousness of these fairy creatures normally functions upon the astral plane which is a life plane. When a more objective self-expression is entered upon, a process of self-clothing in the matter of the ether which is a form plane is more or less instinctively carried out. This culminates in the temporary creation of an etheric body ensouled, interpenetrated and surrounded by the astral creator. The reproduction as relatively fixed forms of currents in the astral aura and the formation of garlands, belts and wands as expressive of attributes are natural processes. They are, I believe, manifestations in the small world of fairy of those Cosmic creative processes and laws by which external Nature comes into existence as an expression of THAT from which it emanates. Admittedly the nature spirit forms are illusory and evanescent, but so is the whole objective universe from the point of view of ultimate reality.

This microcosmic expression of Macrocosmic powers and laws gives even to the smallest forms and beings of nature their profound interest and significance. The chemical atom is thought to reproduce in ultra-microscopic proportions the form and interior movements of a solar system, themselves both manifestations of still greater units and objective expressions of universal numerical and geometrical principles. Similarly, my observations have led me to believe the forms of elf, fairy and dryad are the result of the operation of the laws by which the Cosmos is built. A study of these beings can, therefore, lead the observer from the minute effect to the great Cause, from the single existence to the general principle.

The remarks and descriptions which follow are admittedly limited, both in range and understanding, being taken from records of my first halting attempts to investigate the Kingdom of Fairy. For the sake of accuracy, however, they are presented almost as then written, rather than expanded in the light of later knowledge. If further explanation and even apology be needed for the inclusion of so much of the apparent *trivia* of fairy lore in this work, I would answer that in the light of fuller knowledge the little people may be found to occupy, however unconsciously, positions of importance in the fulfilment of Nature's mysterious plans and processes. The power of the single cell to move, breathe, reproduce and nourish itself and that of groups of cells to communicate, co-operate and co-ordinate their activities in the development of organic bodies, may be explained by the presence and instinctually directive influence of the nature spirits. Amoeba are known to move towards a conjoined, communal existence stimulated and guided physically by certain chemical substances. The origin and action of such substances and of the mechanism apparent in the evolution of the slime moulds and their successors in the scale, may perhaps be traceable to the activities of invisible, astro-etheric organisms of the order of the nature spirits of the four elements.

Nothing in Nature is insignificant. The extremely minute is as important as the inconceivably vast. Dimension and apparent significance in the light of present human knowledge cannot be regarded as standards of importance. Moreover since the smallest atom and the greatest Archangel are produced, shaped and evolved in accordance with the same laws, a study of the minute and the apparently unimportant can lead to a comprehension of all that exists. From this point of view a nature spirit is of as much consequence as a creative God and those who take all Nature for their field of study can hardly afford to neglect these embodiments of Nature's indwelling life. Nature spirits may one day be found to be links in the chain of causation by which a universe is conceived, mentally "named" and its "name" or "word" uttered so that the sound thereof causes the primordial single concept to become manifest as physical nature in all its infinite complexity and variety of evolving beings, species and forms.

I admit that I have also been moved by the thought that readers—and those read to—of tender years may find in these descriptions much that will entertain, and perhaps provide later on an easy gateway to a deeper study of the Kingdom of the Gods. There is, moreover, a further reason for interest in the elementals of earth, water, air and fire which will be apparent to those of my readers who are interested in alchemy.

BROWNIES [1]

The European brownies I have studied, though differing considerably in detail, have always presented certain common characteristics which place them unmistakably in their own family.

A medieval style of attire is generally affected. A short brown coat, sometimes with a wide scalloped collar, bright buttons and facings of green, brown knee-breeches, rough stockings and two distinct kinds of boots are worn. Sometimes a large, heavy "agricultural" boot is seen, and at others a long, pointed, lighter shoe. One way in which variations can occur is suggested in the description given later of the manufacture of a pair of fairy shoes.

A pointed cap is the usual head-dress, though a low-brimmed hat occasionally replaces the nightcap-shape more generally worn. Groups of brownies, apparently believing themselves to be hard at work, have been seen wearing aprons closely resembling those worn by blacksmiths; bright buckles and clasps are generally part of their equipment. Working brownies carry and pretend to use tools, chiefly spades and

---

[1] Part of the subject matter under this and the following headings in this Chapter appeared in my book, *Fairies at Work and at Play*, published by the Theosophical Publishing House, 68 Great Russell Street, London, W. C. 1, by whose kind permission it is included in a revised form in this work.

picks, with which they delve in the earth with great earnestness. Some tribes of brownies are short and squat, with fat, round bodies and short limbs, others being slim and youthful in appearance. Their height varies from some four to twelve inches. Usually the face is that of an old man, with grey eyebrows, moustache and beard, red complexion and a weatherbeaten aspect. The eyes are small and beady and the expression simple and kindly.

By nature they are communicative and friendly creatures, living in tribes and, like most of the fairy peoples, highly imitative of man in their habits, their attire and their methods of work and play. They belong to the soil and have much of the rustic simplicity of the tiller of the ground. What function they perform in the processes of Nature is not clear; [1] they are generally to be found on or just beneath the surface of the ground. I have seen them digging most solemnly amongst the roots of growing plants, yet such an expression of mock seriousness and make-believe pervades all their activities that it is never quite clear whether they regard their endeavour as work or play. The following accounts of nature spirits of earth, water, air and fire are taken from descriptions of scenes observed on different occasions, and may help to an understanding of these little people.

A BROWNIE VILLAGE

On the steep side of one of the crags on the western shores of Thirlmere is a very large colony of brownies; they live a few feet below the ground level and spend their time as much beneath as above the surface. I see a number of small houses, just under the surface of the hill. Quite perfect in shape, with windows and doors, they are scattered irregularly about the hillside, and amongst the leaves, the roots and the rocks which surround them numbers of brownie figures are

[1] Later investigations have brought some additional knowledge concerning the function of the nature spirits. This is included in Part I, Chapter III.

to be seen. The following is an attempt to describe one of
these selected at random.

Not more than six inches high, he looks like a little old
man, wearing a brown hat shaped like a nightcap, and a
brown suit consisting of what appears to be the brownie regu-
lation knickerbockers, stockings and boots. The face is
grey-beared and bears the impress of an ancient rusticity.
Undoubtedly there is the make-believe of domestic life,
though I do not see any female figure in this fairy village.
Brownies literally swarm over this hillside and vary little in
appearance, expression or intelligence. They seem to be just
"evolving" here. They differ from any brownies I have previously seen in that they do not appear to "work" in connection with any processes of Nature; though they venerate the
trees, they do not serve them in any capacity.

One of a younger looking type of nature spirit which
also lives here has now approached me and, standing some
two or three yards on my right, is proceding to display himself with extravagant gestures and simple-minded humour.
He is much slimmer than the older-looking brownies, and
has a touch of colour about him—a little red on the hat (which
is conical with the point hanging back) and a little green in
his costume. I hardly think he can be a brownie; his feet
run down to a point, his nether limbs are thin and elongated
and his hands are too large for the rest of his body. He rests
his left hand on his hip and points with his right hand in the
direction of the wood, as if proudly displaying the beauties
of the place. Added to his pride there is a good deal of vain
glory and childish self-satisfaction. His face is clean-shaven
and red, his eyes small, his nose and chin prominent, his
mouth very wide and still further expanded into a grin. His
gestures and postures are extravagant and amazing. His
body is so supple that he can bend and stretch to almost any
position.

I cannot persuade him to approach any nearer, as when I try to do so he immediately begins to show apprehension. He appears to feel uncomfortable, though not, I think, really afraid. The human aura is inharmonious to him and he would probably lose his equilibrium within it. By contrast I realise how ethereal and fragile is his make-up, possessing less consistency than a puff of wind; yet the form is clearly outlined and the details are sharply defined.[1]

Looking again at the brownie community and striving to grasp some of the details of its life, certain peculiar facts present themselves. For example, an endeavour to see the inside of their houses showed to my surprise that when one "went in at the door" there was nothing there! The outside shape is fairly perfect and quite picturesque, but the inside is just darkness. In fact, the illusion of a house entirely disappears when the consciousness is directed to the interior. Certain fine lines of flowing magnetism are all that one sees. The brownies enter by the door and then put off the brownie form, descending deeper into the earth in a relatively formless state. They all seem to have the conception of being busy, hurrying about the place in a pseudo-serious manner; but to me the whole thing is pure make-believe.

The houses do not belong to any individual or group. Any member of the colony uses them, this "use" being limited merely to passing in and out through the door. They certainly get some satisfaction from contemplating the exterior of these thought-built structures. I do not see, belonging to these woodland brownies, any of the working tools, satchels or aprons which I have noticed on other occasions. They appear to be less intelligent and less highly evolved and far more aimless in their existence than any others I have met.

[1] Later experience suggests that this little fellow was a woodland elf rather than a brownie.

MANUFACTURE OF FAIRY BOOTS

Among the little folk on this hillside facing Helvellyn, the first to be observed is an elderly brownie who, now that we have seated ourselves, steps out to the edge of the firewood behind us. He is some six or eight inches high and wears a long, pointed cap, like a slightly imperfect cone, and a little green jerkin scalloped at the lower edge and falling about his hips; it is edged with brown, fastened with buttons and has a broad, cape-like collar, also scalloped and edged. Little trousers complete his attire. At first he shows the lower limbs of an elf, elongated and pointed. He has a long, grey, scanty beard, and both his face and body are thinner and more austere than those of the usual brownie. He reminds me slightly of a caricature of Uncle Sam, clothed in the constume of Falstaff.

He takes much interest in our dog and fearlessly approaches close to its nose. He appears unable to take in the group as a whole. He realises the presence of human beings, but the first detail which strikes him is the type of boots which I am wearing— canvas-topped, army gum-boots. After looking at mine steadily he proceeds to make himself a very respectable imitation of them, of which he is inordinately proud. His simple mental image is quite sufficient to cover his own feet with a copy of the pair of boots at which he looks so admiringly. After strutting about for a time, as if to get used to them, he finally stalks off into the woods.

ELVES

Elves differ from other nature spirits chiefly in that they are not usually clothed in any reproduction of human attire, and their bodily constitution consists of one solid mass of etheric substance, entirely without interior organisation.

WOOD ELVES

Two tiny wood elves come racing over the ground past us, as we sit on a fallen tree trunk. Seeing us they pull up about five feet away and stand regarding us with considerable amusement, but quite without fear. They appear as if completely covered in a tight-fitting, one-piece skin, which glistens as if wet, and is coloured like the bark of a beech tree. There is a large number of these figures racing about the ground. Their hands and feet are large out of all proportion to the rest of their bodies. Their legs are thin and their ears run upwards to a point, being almost pear-shaped. Their noses, too, are pointed and their mouths wide. No teeth, no structures, exist inside the mouth—not even a tongue, so far as can be seen—just as if the whole were made up of a piece of etheric jelly. A small green aura surrounds them. The two I am specially observing live in the roots of a huge beech tree. Now they disappear through a crevice, into which they walk as one might enter a cave, and sink below the ground to become merged into the etheric double of the tree.

SEASIDE ELVES

Playing on the shore, amongst the seaweed and the stones, are queer little elf-like forms. They have oversize heads, elfish faces, large ears, little round bodies and short, thin legs ending in feet which appear almost web-like. They are from three to six inches in height, are familiar with human beings and are in no way disturbed by their presence. They are apparently concerned with the life and the cell processes of seaweed.

GNOMES

"Gnome" is a generic title for the nature spirits of the element of earth. Investigation shows that while all the types of traditional fairy exist in Nature, there are wide divergences within each type. Some of the differentiations are so great as to call for new names and new classifications. In the future, when doubtless the naturalist, ethnologist and explorer will enter Fairyland and text-books of the Kingdom of Fairy will be studied in every school, special names will of necessity be given to all the many and various kinds of fairy people. As I find the traditional names to be the most satisfactory from many points of view, I have classified such inhabitants of Fairyland as I have studied under the name given to the race they most nearly resemble.

Tree creatures and winged manikins are described under this heading, although they differ in many important particulars from the true gnome. The students may hesitate to accept the existence of a winged gnome which lives in a tree; nevertheless, so far as my observation goes, those I have classed under this heading resemble the gnome more closely than any other type. I shall class as "gnomes", therefore, several creatures which differ in many respects from the gnome of fairy tradition.

The true gnome normally lives within the etheric double of the earth, is usually thin and lanky, grotesque in appearance, cadaverous and lantern-jawed and is sometimes a solitary. He gives the impression of extreme old age; his whole appearance and bearing are utterly different from those of present-day man. His arms are too long for our sense of proportion and, like his legs, are bent at the joints as if they had grown stiff with age. The complexion is very rough and coarse, the eyes are small and black, sloping slightly upwards at the sides. As has been said, the gnome is apparently a relic of the days of ancient Lemuria, and if this is true it may mean that the type is a representation of the appearance of

EARTH GNOME

the peoples of those days. The earth gnome is not a pleasant type of elemental; those met with in England have been either quite black or peat-brown in colour and though I have rarely incurred their active hostility, their atmosphere is decidedly unpleasant.

AN EMBRYO ROCK GNOME

Deep within the solid rock behind us there is an evolving consciousness which manifests chiefly as formless blotches of colour within the otherwise almost colourless elemental essence of the rock—a sort of embryo gnome. The beginnings of a head, with eyes and mouth, are visible in shadowy outline, but the rest of the body is only faintly suggested, like the preliminary work of an artist who might put in his main patches of colour and leave the clear outlines to a later stage. But for this vagueness, the creature would be excessively ugly, not to say monstrous in appearance. To etheric sight, the whole rock is transparent and its inhabitant appears as if within a huge celluloid receptacle, through which it is but hazily aware of its surroundings. The only power of volition that it appears to possess is that of slowly changing the focus and direction of its dim and limited consciousness; this it does very vaguely and dreamily. The presence of this creature gives a certain individuality to the rock, noticeable on the physical plane as specialised magnetic vibration. It is difficult to judge the size of the gnome, but it is probably ten to fifteen feet high. The embryo feet are deep below the surface of the earth in which the rock is buried, and the head some three feet from the top of the rock.

AN ENGLISH FAIRYLAND

Deep in the heart of the Cotswold district of England there is a lovely, verdant valley through which no highway passes. Its name, said to mean "Vale of Peace", truly

indicates one of its greatest charms.   The ubiquitous motor-
bus brings parties of tourists to nearly all the famous beauty
spots of Britain, but not to the Vale of Peace.

The winding valley is perhaps two miles in length.   Its
steep hillsides are partly covered with thick beech-woods,
with here and there a grove of larch and fir.   Dotted about
on the green hillsides are the grey stone cottages and farms
of which the little village consists.   A stream runs through
wood and meadow and flows with gentle murmur past
orchards and cottage gardens to the great world beyond.
Within the valley there is green beauty, a wealth of wild
flowers, seclusion and the peace of the countryside.   The
woodmen's voices and the blows of their axes, the call of
the birds, the lowing of the cattle in the pastures, the sighing
of the trees in the soft breezes, are the only sounds which normally
reach one in summer time when gazing on the restful
scene.   These are blended to form a harmonious undertone,
the song which Nature sings in those places where her beauty
is unspoiled.   Sometimes, on calm and windless summer days,
the valley seems to be steeped in silence and in peace.

TREE MANIKINS

The fairy folk seem less shy of human beings in these
woods and meadows than elsewhere.   The tree nymphs, the
water spirits and the numerous tribes of little brownie men
have not learned as yet to shrink and hide themselves when
man appears.   Playing about on the thick carpet of the beech
leaves of past seasons, with which the ground under the trees
is covered, are hundreds of small brown manikins.   From
eight to twelve inches high, they vary in colour from the grey-
green of the beech trunks to the rich brown of the dead leaves.
Many of them have the faces of old men and they wear coats
and knee-breeches of a material which looks like brown beech
bark.   They have long, pointed feet and some wear tiny boots.

Their facial expression is one of intent seriousness and earnestness—all about nothing.   At first glance one might think that they were very important people, but in looking into what corresponds to their minds—the merest instinct as of young animals or birds—one finds an almost complete blank.

They "live" inside the etheric double of the trees into which there are accepted entrances.   These are generally at small hollows in the trunk, frequently, though not always, level with the ground   There are groups which live up in the forks where the branches leave the main trunk and the etheric currents divide.   Though they can move for a short distance in the air, they seem to prefer to run up the trunks of the trees. This they do as easily as if they ran upon the flat ground. They seem to be unaffected by the law of gravity, for they sometimes maintain a horizontal position with their bodies at right angles to the trunks as they pass up and down.

Although their ether-built forms are a homogeneous "solid", without interior organisations, a close observation of their movements seems to indicate something corresponding to a muscular system.   This is particularly noticeable when they jump, as they often do for short distances, the last half-yard of their journey back to their trees being frequently covered by a leap.   The leg with which the take-off is made certainly seems slightly to harden and stiffen, to relax during flight, and both legs to be braced up for the landing; this is perfectly smooth, the forward movement continuing at practically the same speed.

A great number of these little people have gradually become aware of the presence of our party and, gathered in a semicircular crowd, are observing us from within the wood. Some are sitting as if transfixed; others walk up and down and appear to be addressing remarks to their seated fellows as they pass them.   Others again make little exploratory journeys in our direction, retiring as our auras become too much for them. This contact with us seems slightly to quicken all their faculties, such as they are. Whilst the comparison is not a nice one, the effect is not unlike that of alcohol upon one unaccustomed to it. Though it will die down, it will leave some permanent result upon them—one hopes a quickening of their evolution.

A LANDSCAPE ANGEL

Some gnomes, as far as my observations reveal, eventually evolve into presiding geniuses or gods of areas of countryside of increasing dimensions. A beautiful landscape angel presides over this valley. About twenty feet tall, its brilliant, many-coloured aura, when extended, reaches out to a distance of at least one hundred yards on all sides. Occasionally it is further extended to reach across the valley at its widest, as well as down to the little stream below.

The face is noble and beautiful and the eyes are dazzlingly bright. They are centres of force rather than organs of sight, for they are not used, as are the human eyes, for vision and the expression of thought and emotion. The colours of the aura are brilliant, and change constantly as the auric forces flow in waves and vortices outward from the central form. Now the predominant hue is deep royal blue, with scarlet and golden yellow sweeping across and through it, making eddies and waves of colour as they flow outwards in a continuous stream. Then a background of pale rose appears, with soft nile-green, sky-blue and the palest of yellow shining through. In addition, streams of force flow upwards from the head and shoulders, the most brilliant of these arising from a force centre in the middle of the head, which is the seat of consciousness in the form.

By moving slowly down the valley with extended aura, the angel is able to touch with its auric forces every living thing within it, pouring into each a share of its own stimulating life-force. The hosts of the lesser nature spirits instinctively respond to the quickening impulses from this angel, and I see the brownies, the tree spirits and the fairies answering to its touch as its powers rush out upon them. The elves and the brownies feel a sudden exaltation, the source of which they cannot fully comprehend, though they recognise it as a constant feature of their lives. The fairies feel an added joy under the stimulating influence of the *deva's* outpoured power.

The character of this *genius loci* is an unusual combination of *devic* universality of consciousness and impersonality of outlook with a human comprehension of the needs and the sufferings of man. I feel sure that every birth and death within the valley must be known to this *deva*, and that any pain which might accompany either is eased as far as its powers permit. I see memory thought-forms in the aura, which show the angel taking within its glowing radiance the souls of those who have recently died. I see, too, that it watches the children at play and the old folk taking their ease. It is, indeed, the Guardian Angel of the valley, and happy are those who live within its care. The experiences referred to in the Introduction, which proved so far-reaching in its results, came to me in this delightful place.

The presence of this angel gives a certain quality to the atmosphere, a local characteristic, distinctly noticeable throughout the whole length of the valley, which has a charm amounting to glamour. It must also affect every human being who resides here for any length of time, particularly those who are born and live within the angel's consciousness and the continual play of its aura.

UNDINES

The undine belongs to the subtle element of water and, so far as my experience goes, is never to be found far away from ocean, lake, river, stream and fall. She is definitely feminine in form, is always unclothed, does not usually have wings and only rarely wears any kind of adornment. Her form, whether diminutive or of human stature, is entrancingly beautiful, and her movements are full of grace. The water-fall is one of her favourite haunts and there she is to be seen disporting herself, often with a group of water sprites, enjoying to the full the magnetic forces of the fall.

Apparently there are periods when the undine retires from the vivid, external life in which she is most frequently observed and finds a measure of calm and repose deep down in the still, cool depths of the pools below the falls or in the quieter reaches of the rivers, as well as in lakes and tarns. This peaceful life below the waters is in marked contrast to the intense activity and joy she manifests amid falling water and sunlit spray.

The three fundamental processes of Nature—absorption, assimilation and discharge—are expressed fully in the outer life of the undine; indeed, that life may be said to consist of a continued repetition of those three processes. Poised amid the spray, or in the centre of the downward rushing torrent, she gradually absorbs the vital energy from the sunlight and the magnetism from the fall. As the limit of absorption is reached, in one dazzling flash of light and colour, she releases the energy with which she has become surcharged. At that magical moment of release she experiences an ecstasy and exaltation beyond anything normally possible to mere mortals dwelling in the prison of the flesh. The expression on the face, and particularly in the eyes, is beautiful beyond description. The countenance expresses rapturous joy and a sense of heightened vitality and power, whilst the eyes flash with dazzling radiance. The whole bearing, the perfect form and the brilliant splendour of the auric radiance combine to produce a vision of enchanting loveliness. This condition is immediately followed by one of dreamy pleasure, in which the consciousness is largely withdrawn from the physical world and its etheric counterpart, and centred in the astral world. The undine etheric body becomes vague and indistinct for the time being until, she having enjoyed and assimilated the whole experience, it reappears and the threefold process is repeated. After a time she returns to the quietude of the watery depths.

UNDINES AT A WATERFALL

These water fairies resemble graceful young girls, are entirely unclothed and are probably from eight to twelve inches tall. Their long "hair" streams behind them and they wear a decoration, resembling a garland of small flowers, around their foreheads. They play in and out of the fall, flashing through it from different directions, and calling all the time in wild, unearthly tones. The voice is infinitely remote and reaches me but faintly, like a shepherd's call across some Alpine valley. It is a complex vowel sound, but as yet I cannot easily name the series of vowels of which it is composed. Undines can either travel up the fall against the stream or remain motionless within it, but they generally play and flash through it. When a cloud has passed away from the face of the sun and the fall again becomes brilliantly sunlit, they appear to experience an added joy; the *tempo* of their movements then quickens and their singing becomes more unrestrained. I can most nearly represent their song by the vowels e, o, u, a, i, in one long, plaintive tone which ends with an appealing cadence.

There are between eight and twelve undines of varying heights playing at this fall, the tallest being about twelve inches high. Some of them have rosy-coloured auras, some pale green, and the closer contact I am now obtaining shows me what extremely beautiful creatures they are, and at the same time how utterly remote from the human family. Their etheric bodies pass in and out of the great rocks at the side of the fall without experiencing any obstruction. I am quite unable to attract their attention or to influence them in any way. Some of them pass under the water in the basin at the foot of the fall, and occasionally appear amidst the swirling froth. The garland, referred to previously, is luminous and apparently forms part of their auras.

THE PRESIDING SPIRIT OF A FALL

We are in a bower of bracken and rocks, a veritable fairyland, close to a waterfall in the Lake District of England. The undine of this fall looks like a tall and graceful young girl, unclothed and of singular beauty. She differs in some characteristics from undines previously observed in that she is taller, has a more highly developed intelligence and auric forces flow out behind her in wing-like form as well as on every side. She seems to ensoul the rocks, trees, ferns and mosses, in addition to the waterfall and pools. When first seen, she sprang out of the solid rock—a marvellously beautiful figure—and remained poised for a moment in the air, after which the etheric form disappeared. She repeated this process several times but her presence, whether etherically visible or not, continued to be distinctly felt.

Her whole form is a soft rose pink. The "hair" is fair and shining, the brow broad, the features beautifully modelled, the eyes large and luminous and, whilst their expression has something of the spirit of the wild, their glance is not unkindly. The auric wings are small in proportion to the body and would surely be inadequate for flight, if such had been their purpose; they, too, are of a glowing roseate hue. Even more striking than the form is the rainbow-like aureole which surrounds her, as a halo sometimes seems to surround the moon. This aura is almost spherical in shape and consists

of evenly arranged, concentric spheres of colour, too numerous and in far too rapid movement for detailed description.
It would seem to contain all the colours of the spectrum in
their palest shades, with rose, green and blue predominating.
Some of the spheres of colour are outlined with a golden fire
and beyond the outer edge a shimmering radiance of pearly
white gives added beauty to the aureole and lovely form within. Over the head a powerful upward flow of forces inter-
penetrates the aura in a fan-shaped radiation. This appears
to come from a point in the middle of the head, where there
is a brilliant golden centre, slightly below the level of the eyes
and midway between them. The whole region of the fall is
vibrant with her life.

LAKE SPIRITS

At different parts of the surface of Lake Thirlmere, which
lies beneath us, numbers of nature
spirits of the element of water are
to be seen skimming swiftly over the
surface, generally at a height of some
six or eight feet, but sometimes rising
much higher. Although they usually
remain over the water, they make
occasional flights above the fields. They somewhat resemble
large, white birds flying at great speed. At this distance I
cannot make out any distinct shape, for they assume and dis-
card many different, bird-like forms with great rapidity.
There is a permanent suggestion of a wing-like formation of
the aura, and sometimes the likeness of a human face and
head.

PRIMITIVE
SEA NATURE SPIRIT

FAIRIES

In order to help the reader to visualise clearly the
appearance of a fairy when materialised, I recommend the

study of the fairy photographs in Sir Arthur Conan Doyle's book *The Coming of the Fairies* and E. L. Gardner's book *Fairies*.[1] I am personally convinced of the *bona fides* of the two girls who took these photographs. I spent some weeks with them and their family, staying in their home, and became assured of the genuineness of their clairvoyance, of the presence of fairies exactly like those photographed in the glen at Cottingley, and of the complete honesty of all parties concerned.

In order that such photographs could be taken, the fairies had to be materialised, presumably by an invisible Adept operator; for only thus could they reflect actinic light. In this process of densification, the true nature of the fairy form was concealed beneath the covering of etheric and tenuous, reflective, physical substance. The photographs show, in consequence, apparently solid, fleshy forms, clothed with transparent garments. At the astral level, the fairy body is at once seen to be without solid substance, to consist of streams of flowing energies which might give, especially at first glance, the illusory appearance of a fixed shape.

The human mind inevitably tends to give to its perceptions familiar forms. In consequence, unless great care is taken, every appearance of solidity will present itself to the mind-brain of seers, and generally without their being in the least aware of the process and its effects. The observer must, in consequence, be constantly on guard against this action of the mind and try to see and record the reality, however unusual it may appear. Although I have thus tried, I cannot guarantee the complete absence of error in my descriptions.

DRYADS

The mento-emotional counterparts of woods are often filled with entrancing interest and beauty. The life forces

[1] The Theosophical Publishing House, 68 Great Russell Street, London,

from the plant kingdom and other emanations from the trees, particularly the larger ones, fill the atmosphere with fine radiations amidst which the tree nature spirits play and angels live and move. The latter sometimes give the impression of a rather dreamy state of consciousness and of being themselves expressions of tree life, one with the ensouling spirit of all the vegetation. They merge into and emerge from the trees, glide about the wood rather like tall, somewhat shy maidens, slender, graceful and robed in diaphanous garments of many shades of green. A description may serve as illustration:

The tree fairies and higher nature spirits inhabiting a wood near Kendal, in Westmorland, are truly beautiful. They move about amongst the trees with a gentle, quiet grace. One of them whom I think has observed us and does not seem to be afraid, slightly raises her light, filmy garment, through which the rosy form can faintly be seen. The "hair" is long and tiny lights play like a garland around her head. So beautiful is her carriage that, were it not for the complete absence of self-consciousness and the perfect candour shown in the expression of face and eyes, I should have thought she was posing. All around are others equally beautiful, each differing in some slight degree from her fellows, and many of them far less outward-turned in consciousness. Another, whose back is toward me, has lovely, long, dark "hair", which hangs well below the waist. One slender white arm is stretched out before her, a little to the side, as she glides slowly through the wood. They often seem to be less nature spirits with separate identities than the souls of the trees, as it were nature spirit expressions of the evolving tree life; for they blend themselves with the larger trees, disappearing from view for a time, later to re-emerge and move about the wood.

Similes can prove misleading but, when watching the nature spirits and angel inhabitants of wood and forest, they sometimes appear before one as would fishes floating out of ocean depths into clear focus for a few moments and then receding, to be lost as if merged once more with their watery element. The more advanced tree angels, those associated with very old and large trees, exhibit a more human clarity of mental outlook and power. Their gaze can be keen and penetrating as they turn their attention upon one who enters their realm and is able to see and communicate with them. Nevertheless, in their case also the impression is received of an intimate blending of their life and consciousness with that of the tree which they ensoul, and the evolution of which they assist.

FAIRY GLAMOUR

On one occasion, whilst studying the nature spirit life in the countryside of Lancashire, a somewhat advanced nature spirit of air associated with the plant kingdom provided an interesting display of the glamorous influence which certain kinds of fairies are able to throw over one who approaches their domain. My record of the experience reads:

A beautiful and highly developed fairy is associated with a briar hedge on which wild roses are blooming in profusion. She is of an especially engaging character and in stature is some four feet tall. Lightly robed in a flowing, transparent, filmy, auric garment, she regards us with the friendliest of smiles. Her aura is noticeably vital and looks like a cloud of many soft yet radiant hues, through which shafts of dazzling light flash and radiate. The colours include soft, luminous pale rose, pale green, lavender and misty blue,

FAIRY JOY

throughout which shoot the brilliant lances of light. She is in a state of exalted happiness.

As an experiment, I yielded partially to the enchantment which she deliberately exercised and to the appealing call with which she invited, nay even challenged me to forsake the world

of men and share with her, and others of her kin hovering near, the irresponsible gaiety of the Kingdom of Fairy. For a time, almost unconscious of the body yet always sufficiently awake in it to return at will, I experienced some measure of the joyful, care-free radiant happiness which seems to be the permanent condition of all the dwellers in the fairy world. There is danger in too close a contact;[1] for it requires a decided effort to withdraw and take up the burden—as it then seemed—of physical existence once again.

A FAIRY INVITATION

FAIRIES AND GRASS ELVES

The surface of this field is densely populated by fairies, brownies and a species of tiny elves associated with grass. The fairies float through the air, assuming graceful poses and expressing in the highest degree the qualities of lightheartedness and gaiety. A number of them are flitting about singly, pausing a moment between each flight and bearing in their hands something which they appear to give to the plants and flowers at each of their stopping places. They stretch out their hands as if applying vital forces to the plants, the etheric doubles of which glow in consequence and then move swiftly away again. They are definitely feminine in appearance,

Vide *La Belle Dame Sans Merci*, Keats.

dressed in white or very pale rose coloured, shimmering material of exceedingly fine texture. This is drawn in at the waist and shines like mother-of-pearl. The auric wings, when etherically materialised, are small and oval in shape.

The elves are from three to six inches in height. They are little, force-built figures, shining with a green light, and look as if they were clothed with a single close-fitting grass-green garment. Their faces are chubby and child-like. The eyes have a somewhat arch expression and they are wholly absorbed in the short, swinging flights with which, alone and in groups, they move about the field. Occasionally the currents of force in their auras seem to join and cross above the head, giving to some of them the appearance of being horned. They are associated with

GRASS ELF

the ensouling life in the cells of the grass and other plants and presumably play some part, however small, in its enclosure in form.

DANCING FAIRIES, COTTINGLEY

A bright radiance suddenly shines out over the field, some sixty yards away. It is due to the arrival of a group of fairies under the control of a superior fairy, who is autocratic and definite in her orders, holding unquestioned command. They spread themselves out into a gradually widening circle around her, and as they do so a soft glow shines over the grass. Since they swung high over the tree tops and down into the field, the circle has spread to approximately twelve feet in width. Each member of this fairy band is connected by a stream of light with the directing fairy, who is in the centre and slightly above them. These streams are of different shades of yellow, deepening to orange; they meet in the centre, merging in her aura, and there is a constant flow backwards and forwards along them. The form produced by this is something like an inverted opalescent, glass fruit dish, with the central fairy as the stem and the lines of light, which flow in graceful, even curves, forming the sides of the bowl. The impression was received, that the interchanges and the complex designs produced by the dance which followed stimulated, and provided a model for, the development of forms in the plant kingdom of Nature in the neighbourhood.[1]

LAKE DISTRICT

A group of fairies is gambolling and dancing on a small plateau on the side of the Wythburn stream. Their bodies, some six inches in height, are feminine in appearance. Their clothing is chiefly pale blue and their "wings", which are similarly coloured and almost oval in shape, are constantly fluttering as they dance in a circle, hand in hand. Some of them wear a loose girdle from which is suspended an instrument like a horn. All are draped with a material which serves to conceal the roseate form more completely than is usual with this type of nature spirit. Their "hair", which in all cases is brown, varies from very light to quite dark shades.

They are carrying out a concerted movement which resembles a country dance and I think it must be their thought and their movements that cause numbers of small, astro-etheric daisy-like flowers to appear and disappear near the ground, within and around the circle, sometimes singly and sometimes as wreaths or chains. They are also discharging

---

[1] Later studies have confirmed this early impression. Vide Part III, Chapter III, " The Fairy Builders of Form ", *et seq.*

into the surrounding atmosphere a specialised energy in the form of silver sparks, and an entrancingly beautiful effect is produced by this miniature electrical display flowing through their auras and the luminous mist in which the whole group is bathed. This mist extends to a height of probably eight or ten inches above their heads and reaches its highest point over the centre of the group. The effect of it upon the fairies is to give them the sense of complete seclusion. In fact, no nature spirit in the neighbourhood enters the charmed sphere.

The fairy dancers have now changed their formation and are going through an evolution of considerable intricacy, making radial "chains" across the circle. This does not remain in the same place, and when the group moves the secluding aura moves with it. The dance, which is also a ritual, resembles certain figures in the *Lancers*. The fairies have a decided sense of rhythm, for although their movements are spontaneous and free, they are to some extent keeping time.

As I watch them, there develops slowly in the centre of the circle a rose-coloured, heart-shaped form whose pulsations discharge the silvery force, which flows out in fine lines or striations. The auric encasement has now increased considerably in size and is not unlike a large, inverted glass bowl. They seem to have some idea that they are creating or building a definite shape, for radial divisions, extremely thin and glittering, have been built, dividing the tenuous form into compartments. Gradually the group drifts away out of range of my vision, having doubtless carried out some formative function on behalf of the plant kingdom.

A FAIRY QUEEN

We are surrounded by a group of joyous, dancing fairies. The leader is some two feet tall, clothed in transparent, flowing

draperies, and has a star on her forehead. She has large,
glistening "wings" of delicate shades of pink and lavender.
Her "hair" is light golden brown and streams behind her,
merging with the other flowing forces of her aura. The form
is perfectly modelled and rounded, like that of a young girl,
and the right hand holds a wand. Her face is stamped with
a decided impress of power, especially noticeable in the clear
blue eyes which, on occasion, glow as with living fire. Her
brow is broad, her features small and rounded, the tiny ears
a poem of physical perfection. The bearing of head, neck
and shoulders is queenly, the whole pose being full of grace.
A pale blue radiance surrounds this beautiful creature, while
golden flashes of light play around and above her head. The
lower portion of the aura is shell pink, irradiated with
white light.

She is aware of our presence, seems to understand my
purpose, and has graciously remained more or less motionless
for this description. She holds up her wand, which is about
the length of her forearm and is white and shining, glowing
at the tip with a golden light. I hear faint, far-away music,
too ethereal to capture, such music as might be given forth
by diminutive, pendant needles, delicately tuned and struck
with tiny hammers. It is more a series of tinkles than a con-
secutive melody, possibly because I am unable fully to catch
the sound. Perchance it is a far-off echo of divine creative
song, the music of the Voice, thus audible deep down in these
etheric regions of the physical world. Now the whole group
rises into the air and vanishes.

SYLPHS

Above the high moorlands of Lancashire, revelling in
the force of the wind, large numbers of angels and nature
spirits of air are to be seen. These sylphs are rather below
human height, but quite human in form, though asexual.

They are disporting themselves wildly in groups of two and
three, travelling at great speed across
the sky.   There is a certain fierceness
in their joy as they call to each other,
their cries sounding like the whistling
of the wind, reminiscent of the call
of the Valkyries in Wagner's opera
of that name.

At first sight they appear to be
winged a pair of magnificent white
pinions being attached to the body
from the top of the shoulders and
reaching down to the feet.   One even
seems to detect a regular, feather-
like formation within these "wings".

SYLPH

This is, however, an illusion produced by the forces flowing
through their auras.   Pale shades of rose and azure blue predominate, while a radiant light of many hues plays continually
about their heads.   A group of three, which I am especially
watching, presents a most spectacular appearance.   As they
wheel and fly across the wide arch of the heavens, brightly
coloured forces flash with extreme rapidity between and all
about them, but more especially in the air above. Occasionally,
variegated sheets of colour, arranged in shining bands, stream
from one sylph to the other.   These are chiefly pale blue, rose,
green and lavender, through which golden, flame-like energies
continually scintillate. There is a definite order in this colour
communication, the meaning of which is hidden from me,
though the chief notes seem to be fierce exultation and joy.[1]

The faces of these astro-mental creatures of the air are like
those of strangely beautiful but fierce Amazons, strong, vital,
and controlled despite their apparently reckless abandon.

---

[1] These early studies were later followed by fuller investigations, from which a measure
of additional information was gained. Vide Part II, Chapter III.

Their movement through the air is very rapid, for they appear to travel distances of ten to fifteen miles in a moment of time.

STORM SYLPHS

While I watched from the slopes of Helvellyn the approach of dark masses of storm-cloud, I observed a number of bird-like air spirits travelling in front of the on-coming clouds. Many of these sylphs are dark and fearsome to look upon, being slightly suggestive of large, swiftly swooping bats. They are darting backwards and forwards across the Wyth-burn valley, sometimes following quite closely the conforma-tion of the hills. They appear to be in a condition of high excitement and give the impression that they are intensifying the electric and magnetic conditions characteristic of a storm. Their faces are human and fully formed, though their expres-sion is distinctly unpleasant. There are large numbers of them—probably a hundred—including some whiter varieties of sylph. They utter a weird, shrieking noise and occasion-ally shoot vertically upwards, passing into the clouds and reappearing above them.

THE GREAT STORM IN LONDON [1]

Demoniacal and terrific beyond description are the be-ings who, high in the aerial regions, are to be seen exulting in the fury of the storm as the jagged flashes of the lightning and the deafening roar of the thunder continue hour after hour through the night. Their appearance faintly resembles that of gigantic bats. Their bodies are human in shape, yet it is no human spirit which shines through those large, upward slanting eyes. Their colour is black as night, red and flame-like, the aura which surrounds them dividing into two huge pinions behind the central form. The "hair" streams back from the head like tongues of flame. Thousands of beings, of whom this is but a halting description, revel in the power

[1] July 10th, 1923.

of the storm. The clash of the mighty forces produces in them intense exaltation of consciousness as they soar, hover, dart, wheel and swoop, apparently intensifying the forces of the storm which in them seem to find embodiment.

Behind these and above them, in the very heart of the tempest, is one beside whom the elementals of storm and disintegration are but as fluttering bats. There, in the midst of it all, is to be seen one of the great *devas* of the elements, human in form, yet in beauty, majesty and power like unto an exalted superman. The knowledge of this presence inspired courage and calmness when, just before a flash of lightning cleaved the heavens with a ribbon of fire, one of the dark beings seemed to swoop down and for a moment hover threateningly, close above us. The baleful eyes, gleaming with frenzy, were fixed upon the earth below. For a fraction of a second the consciousness behind those eyes was touched, producing a feeling of vertigo and terror such as had not been experienced since the days and nights of the first World War. Under this present test the value of those trials was realised, for automatically the will overcame the fear and stilled the trembling of the body, caused by the vision and the deafening crack of thunder by which it was accompanied. Then the dark storm-fiend sped away, uttering the weird, exulting, unearthly cry of his kind, which was continually audible throughout the storm.

In the midst of all this uproar was a calm, an unshakeable poise, a power acknowledged even by these unruly legions. Beyond a certain limit they could not go, for they were ever held in check by the will of that Lord of the Storm who reigned supreme over the elemental forces.

SALAMANDERS

Since, like their relatively formless element, nature spirits of fire are without a fixed form, descriptions of them are somewhat difficult to obtain and record. The suggestion is received of an underlying human shape, limbs and "hair" being built of streams of rushing fiery energy and only rarely conforming in shape and position to the human frame.

The face, however, when not veiled by auric flames, is

distinctly human in appearance. Quite non-human, however, is its expression, whilst the upward-slanting eyes seem to be lit with a kind of unholy delight in the destructive power of their element. The face is triangular, chin and ears being pointed, and the head surrounded and outlined by flickering, orange-red flamelets, through which shoot flashing tongues of fire. Salamanders vary in height from two or three feet to the great colossi of fire-power who are the Fire Lords associated with the sun. The

SALAMANDER

description which follows, although not of Lesser but of Greater Gods, and included here for the sake of continuity in the study of the four elements and their denizens, is taken from the Introduction to and Chapter IV of my book, *The Angelic Hosts*.[1]

I seemed to be standing with him (the angel teacher referred to in the Introduction to the present book) submerged in a sea of fire, which was homogeneous and all-pervasive, yet translucent and transparent. I seemed also to see the sunflower formation of the fire aspect of the Solar Logos and His System, as if the angel and I were standing on one of the petals. Though the distances and dimensions of this fire-world were so colossal as to be physically incomprehensible and beyond measure, yet at this level they were well within

[1] The Theosophical Publishing House, London.

my grasp, and the fact that I was standing completely submerged in a veritable cataract of flame as it rushed past and
swirled about me, did not prevent me from seeing the whole
of it and its shape, as if I were also looking down upon it from
above. I could trace its source in the sun and see its limits
where the tip of a petal touched the Ring-Pass-Not, or edge,
of the System. I was not able to discover the relation of the
physical sun to the fiery sun, but the relative size and luminosity were such that the physical sun would be almost lost in
its fiery counterpart.

Under the angel's guidance I moved about within this
world of fire but, however great the distance we covered, the
same aspect always presented itself. Whether we rose or
fell in the sea of fire, or crossed a wide area of flame, the System
continued to appear like a sunflower presenting its full face
towards us. Contradictory though this may sound, it will
be intelligible to those who are familiar with the idea of the
fourth dimension. At the fire-level, however, the apparent
directions of space, or characteristics revealed by superphysical
cognition, are more than four.

The appearance of the solar Fire Lords was glorious and
awe-inspiring. Their stature must be gigantic. Though they
did not approach the size of the main petals themselves, as
they stood like an inner corolla round the central fiery heart
of the flower they were large enough to be noticeable from
points near the outer edge of the System. When we
approached the centre, they were seen to be solar colossi, and
at one of our resting places a single Fire Lord completely
filled the field of vision. Their forms were definitely human,
though every cell in their bodies resembled a roaring furnace,
while flames leapt and played about them continuously. I
was not able to see their faces with any distinctness and their
eyes were shaded from my view—perhaps by a merciful pro-
vidence—but I received the impression of beauty quite as

strongly as I received that of power. Their beauty was not so much that of shape and form, though their bodies are inexpressibly beautiful. Rather does it belong to the abstract ideal of beauty which they embody. In the fire-world I perceived beauty in the abstract as a living power, equally potent with fire, and realised that as there is a fire aspect of God, so is there a beauty aspect, equal to that of fire in its regenerating, transforming and destructive effects, equally glorious, equally terrible, equally dangerous to him who gazes upon its naked power. I begin to appreciate the truth of the saying that no man may see God and live. Man may climb the heights of the spiritual mountain and the beauty of God may transfigure him, but unless he is prepared for its resistless power, he may be utterly destroyed.[1] In the world of fire there seems to be a highly organised system whereby such dangers are made as remote as possible. The illimitable power, glory and beauty of the Logos pass through the Angelic Hierarchy, which serves as a transformer to reduce and temper them so that forms are built instead of destroyed and dwellers at lower levels are not blinded by their awful might.

The Archangels of Fire dwell amidst these forces and direct the play of the fiery, solar energies according to the will of that supreme Lord of Fire who is the Source of their existence. They are the Gods of Fire, the Archangels of Flame, the spiritual regenerators of the System. Living embodiments of fire-power, they are Viceregents of the Supreme Ruler, of whom both Solar System and Lords of Fire are expressions. All golden and flamelike, they resemble gigantic men built of flame, in the hand of each a spear and on the head a golden crown of living fire. Flames shoot forth from them on every side. Every change of consciousness sends forth tongues of flame, each gesture a flood of fire.

---

[1] Only as far as his personal individuality is concerned, the Dweller in the Innermost being immortal, eternal, indestructible.

Power passes through them, transformed lest its naked force should destroy the very system which, by their mediation, it recreates, regenerates and transforms. They shield the Solar System lest the fiery energy should blind the eyes of those to whom it is a source of light, burn those to whom it is a source of heat, and shatter those to whom it is a source of power. Such in small part are the Mighty Ones who stand before the fiery throne of the Father of Angels and of Men. Below them, rank on rank, are ranged the Gods of Fire. Youngest amongst them are the nature spirits of their elements, the salamanders, Lords of Fire in-the-becoming.

PART III

THE SEPHIROTH

CHAPTER I

THE ANGELS
OF WILL, WISDOM AND INTELLIGENCE

UNIVERSES are formed and permeated by an infinite, creative, vitalising and transforming deific Power which, in Tibetan, is called *Fohat*. This One Life contains within itself infinite potentialities for the production of universes, beings and forms. It has two modes of existence, one passive, one active. During the reign of the passive mode, from the objective point of view, darkness alone exists. The processes of emergence, densification, evolution and transformation of universes, beings and forms into spiritual states occur during the period of activity. These two phases, the passive and the active, alternate ceaselessly throughout eternity. In the world's cosmogonies they are known as Nights and Days.

At the opening of the creative period, the principle of Ideation inherent in the One Life becomes manifest as Universal Mind or divine Intelligence. This is not yet a Being, but a power which awakens from boundless Space at the fructifying touch or "breath" of the One Life. Within Universal Mind, localised or focussed areas of divine Thought appear. These are the "nuclei" within the first "thought cell" of a universe, from which emanate creative impulses. They are not yet individual Beings, though they contain the potentiality of all beings.

137

The process of emanation continues, the first to emerge being the Sephiras, the Numerations, the divine Creative Intelligences. These combine under numerical law to carry out the designs included within divine Ideation. The highest Archangels, from whom in turn the Angelic Hosts emerge, are included within such Emanations. Angels are thus Mind-born Emanations from Absolute Life and the nearer in time and condition to Absoluteness, the greater the beings.. Thus hierarchy is part of the established order of Creation. At the summit of the ladder of angelic existence are the primordial Sephirothal Intelligences, the Archangels of the Face, the Mighty Spirits before the Throne. These are the First Born, the highest, greatest—save for the Primal Embodiment of Universal Mind—manifestations of Creative Intelligence and Power in the Universe. They are everlasting, existing from dawn to eve of Creative Day. At the other end of the scale of angelic existence are the last born, the minute lives emergent from the ocean of Life, the Sephiras in miniature, the nature spirits.

THE SONS OF WILL

Within this hierarchically-ordered race of beings are at least seven main divisions, classified according to the predominant power manifest in each. The Sephira of Will gives birth to innumerable, but not unnumbered, "sons", each in its turn the parent of a vast progeny, all imbued with the fire of the omnipotent Will. Their attribute is power and they are agents for the manifested will of that summation of the Sephiras which is the Logos of the Universe. Invested with cosmic power, robed in white radiance, these parent "Morning Stars" shine more brightly than a thousand suns. They are creators in that the creative ray, the *fohatic* "dart", the arrow of Eros, is by them as "bowmen" directed to its mark, which in the beginning is that region of space in which the universe is to appear. Throughout its formation and growth they continue to direct the fiery ray which, "bursting" into innumerable, whirling shafts of force brings atoms into being. Primordial atoms are of one kind alone. They form the upper layer of each of the seven degrees of density of matter of which the seven worlds or planes are formed. Different atomic combinations form different substances or chemical elements in both the noumenal and phenomenal aspects of the universe. The atom-forming power is *Fohat*. The directors of the process are the Sephira of Will and its Emanations.

In full self-consciousness, the Will-Archangels wield this mighty power. In diminishing degrees, angels of will perform their parts. Pure instinct guides the nature spirits in their functions as servants of the One Will. These are the gnomes, the elementals of earth.

THE SONS OF WISDOM

The Sephira of Wisdom and its "sons" embody and make manifest the principles of cohesion, balance, harmony, inherent in *Fohat* and all that it creates. They also direct the vitalising currents of solar energy by which atomic combinations, molecules, substances and forms are given co-ordination and life. They are called Sons of Wisdom, because Intelligences which blend and harmonise are ever wise. They consciously maintain the balanced equipoise of Nature's several and diverse parts. Each enfolds vast regions within its aura and serves as both vehicle and container for outrushing and returning *fohatic* shafts of power.

These activities of the Sons of Wisdom and other Sephiras were portrayed in the language of the Mysteries as creative intercourse, lawful or unlawful, between Gods and Goddesses and as the progeny supposedly produced. Sephirothal functions and the resulting natural phenomena were thus explained by allegory and fable which, revealing the sacred truths to the sanctified, concealed them from the profane. For such has ever been the method of the Mysteries.

Angels of Wisdom serve in regions of lesser dimensions and deeper density. Nature spirits of water as a subtle element, the great container and conductor in Nature, instinctively play their parts in the outermost regions and densest states of substance in the universe.

THE SONS OF INTELLIGENCE

The Thought that slept as a potency throughout creative Night awoke at Dawn to find embodiment in the most tenuous of all substance, pre-atomic Space. When, thereafter, *Fohat* formed the first atoms, Mind directed their formation. When atoms blended into denser substance, Mind ordered the pattern of their cohesion. When elements appeared, it was Mind that conceived them. When forms followed, Mind fashioned them according to a transcendental "dream" from which it had awakened at Dawn. Mind is the Artist-Craftsman of the universe.

The Sephira of Mind, through and from itself, brought forth innumerable progeny, the Angelic Hosts of Mind from which, in their turn, came forth sylphs and nature spirits, fairies and all the aerial hosts. These serve the Universal Mind. These fashion Nature's outer garb. These conceive and, plane by plane, mentally project the Archetypes, until the densest world is reached and earthly forms appear.

The Universal Mind is omnipresent. With the Egyptians, the God Tehuti, Sephira of Thought and Law, was its symbol and embodiment, preceding in time yet standing behind the creative Logos, ram-headed Amen Ra. Upon his palette he both calculates and records the cosmic cycles and the Nights and Days of Ra. Even *Fohat* is obedient to the Sephira of Thought, the Lord of Number and of Law.

GODS AND GODDESSES

Each Sephira is assisted by its twin. Every Archangel has its counterpart which is the animate "shadow" of itself, its duplicate. All Gods thus have Goddess consorts who are spiritual embodiments and expressions of their powers, just as the Gods themselves are in their turn embodied Universal Power in one or more of its many aspects. The last three of the seven Sephiras are the reflections of the first three, their Goddesses, though each is a mighty individual Intelligence which, in this and preceding universes, has evolved to its present high degree.

Each of the seven Sephiras is an Official, appointed to an office in the government of the universe. Each is a specialist in one group of creative activities, an expert in creative processes, with special powers in one of the seven "fields".

Sephirothal Intelligences are great beyond the comprehension of man. Will and thought are virtually omnipotent in them. By means of these two agencies they establish and maintain throughout creative Day those regions within the circumscribed field at which sun and planets will later be built. Throughout the periods of densification from pure Spirit-Matter to physical sun and globes, and the subsequent progressive etherealisation back to the original pure state, the concentration by which these phenomena are produced is perfectly sustained. Perpetually creating according to numerical law by the action of unified will-thought, the Sephiras are the motionless Lords whose concentration is unbroken and unwavering throughout the whole period of creative activity.

CHAPTER II

THE ANGELS
OF BEAUTY, MIND AND FIRE

THE first three Sephiras, those of Will, Wisdom and Intelligence, are the primaries. The last three are their secondaries. The fourth represents the linking principle between these two groups. The power of the three primaries and the "responses" of the three secondaries all pass through the intermediate fourth Sephira. The interplay between such mighty Powers, the interflow between the three spiritual and three material Sephiras, sets up a stress in the interspace. Lines of force are formed in primordial substance, and it is these which provide the major and minor Archetypes, the living geometrical models upon which all forms are founded.

The fourth Sephira is therefore an Official of supreme significance. Amid the creative stress it must maintain the predetermined "forms", the parent and the offspring Archetypes. Maintenance of rhythm and of pre-chosen frequencies of oscillation in the interplay between the apparently opposing primaries and secondaries, are the preoccupation of the fourth Sephira and its subordinates. All the powers, attributes, offices and activities of the six Sephiras must be possessed and mastered by the fourth, which has to contain and direct them according to numerical Law. The mind of man perceives products of these labours of the fourth Sephira as the order and the beauty of the universe.

142

In concentric spheres from the innermost to the outermost, or from the topmost rung of the sephirothal ladder to its lowest, the fashioners of forms labour in the workshop-studio, which is the objective universe. Their tool is creative fire; their medium creatively impregnated substance. The Source of the power and the genius with which they work is creative Intelligence, active also in both tool and medium. From the centre to the arm-tips of the fiery, six-armed cross [1] formed of the six paths followed by the forthgoing and returning creative energy, the fourth Sephira and its Emanations are omnipresent and ceaselessly at work.

The Contemplative Lord itself stands at the centre whence all arms radiate, all force arises. From it all force flashes and to it all force returns. Archangels and angels have their stations along the arms at increasing distances from the naked power. Nature spirits, like dancing motes within a beam, dwell at the outer ends. Yet all are one. Archangels, angels and nature spirits are but emanations and embodiments of the One Life within their own sephirothal Source. Being thus at one, all are moved solely by impulses arising in that Source and are obedient to a single sephirothal thought and will.

THE SEPHIRA OF MIND-FORMS

The fifth Sephira and all its Hosts are the first conceivers of evolving forms. Through the mind of this mighty One, the divine Ideations pass from the archetypal to the concrete state. Time, the deceiver, confines the limitless and the timeless within that prison-house, the "walls" of which are built of thousands of centuries. Past, present and future imprison therein that divine Thought which for the third Sephira is durational, for the second is everlasting and for the first is eternal. With one foot, as it were, in time and one in

[1] Vide Part II, Chapter II, p. 70 *et seq.*

timelessness, the fourth Sephira links the form and the form-less states, makes possible the transference of divine Ideation from the non-evolving Archetype into myriads of evolving forms. At first these local, temporal forms are faulty, crude and imperfect. At last they are faultless, finished, flawless.

The processes of perfecting forms are directed by the fifth Sephira, beneath whom, rank upon rank, labour Arch-angels, angels and nature spirits. These beings do not create the forms. Divine Ideation from within the One Life, through the third Sephira, gives birth to parental Archetypes. These "breathe" upon the virgin waters of lower space and "speak" the archetypal "Word". Space conceives and slowly brings forth the separate forms, the potentiality of which resides for ever in divine Thought.

These first, time-prisoned forms, life-filled and develop-ing, appearing as if spontaneously in the mind-stuff of the universe, are immediately subjected to two processes by the fifth Sephira and its Hosts. Their shape is improved and, in successive cycles, they are projected into the astral and physi-cal regions where the sixth and seventh Sephiras preside. There they are perfected and hardened, polished and densified by the combined activities of the last three Sephiras and their Hosts. They first appear as thought-forms, imperfect, ill-formed. Life-filled and with dawning sentiency, they are clothed in denser substance. Fully hardened or manifest as densest physical, like plaster models cast in bronze, their deepest density is in course of time attained. Thus are born planets. Ultimately, they die and disintegrate; but their life and ideal forms are preserved and projected anew into their successors.

The sephirothal labours do not cease. The perfection implicit within the imperfect dominates the resistant sub-stance. Matter becomes more malleable, thought more formative, life more sentient, as forms improve. Eventually thought becomes omnipotent. The sevenfold sephirothal "Word" is then "made flesh" and finally in full perfection "dwells among us", or is made materially manifest.

The fifth Sephira is thus responsible for the mental reproduction in form of abstract creative Ideation, which has passed through the archetypal stage under the third Sephira. This all-inclusive, single thought-form, which divides into myriads of separate forms, must be mentally maintained throughout *Manvantara*. No break in the concentration of the will-thought of the fifth Sephira must mar the projection and evolution to perfection of the universe of concrete forms.

Divine thought is embodied in this mighty One. He is Lord of Mind, the embodiment of the directive Intelligence of the "formal" universe. In one sense he is the universe of thought, the One Mind, and of him all other minds are part, being contained within him and being expressions of himself. The power of this Being is that of Universal Will expressed as thought, or *Fohat-Atma-Manas.*[1]

THE ELEMENT OF FIRE

The third Sephira is the innermost Soul of the fifth, which is its manifested Power. Fire is their element. The third Sephira is as white heat, the fifth is as its flame-like radiation. Actually there is neither heat nor flame above the physical world. Hot masses and rising flames, caused physically by combustion of certain elements, have no superphysical counterparts. There is no superphysical burning of substance with consequent change of form. Physical fire and flame are the denser counterparts of a subtle universal element, the intelligence, power and activity of which are those of the third and fifth Sephiras. This is a mystery and more may not here be said, except that physical flame is a temporary and local

---

[1] *Fohat-Atma-Manas*, Cosmic, Creative Electricity-Will-Thought.

manifestation of the deific Presence, and more particularly of the third and fifth Aspects and Emanations of Deity. Each divine Aspect is outwardly manifest as a Being, an Intelligence whose full nature is beyond human comprehension, save in states of lofty contemplation when divine Immanence is perceived and the divine Transcendence intuitively discerned.

Fire on earth, then, is an expression of divine Intelligence, a localised manifestation of Universal Mind: it is that one of the four modes of manifestation on the physical plane which constitutes the electro-magnetic "soul" of physical substance. The somewhat conical, tongue-like shape of a flame is symbolical of this third Aspect of Deity, for in vertical section it is triangular. The triangle is the archetypal "form" of the fire element, and therefore of the third Sephira.

The fifth Sephira transfers the Fire Aspect of Deity to the formal world, where in man it becomes manifest mentally as thought-power, emotionally as desire and physically as heat. In all the varied expressions of the Fire Aspect in Nature and in man, the fifth Sephira is intimately involved as the ensouling Being who is the Mind of Nature.

The process of physical combustion which produces the impressions of fire, flame and heat upon the senses and mind of man excites into hyper-activity the superphysical noumenon of fire, the Fire Aspect of Deity preponderant in the fifth Sephira. This ensouling fire-principle of Nature has its major embodiment in that Being and in his brother, the third Sephira, who is the noumenon of the noumenon, the soul of the soul, of physical fire.

The fifth Sephira, in its turn, is composed of and manifested as innumerable Fire-Gods, Archangels, angels and nature spirits. This vast Host is in perpetual creative activity, continually occupied in the tranference of the *fohatic* fire, the cosmic creative fire-force, from its primal source throughout the five planes of present manifestation.

The fire of *Fohat* is the agent whereby "virgin" matter is made responsive to and reproductive of the archetypal products of divine Ideation. Cosmic fire, which is no burning flame or heat but a form of electrical energy, is the impregnating agency by the action of which root Substance produces universes and all which they contain. The nature and the shape of those products are decided by a combination of numerical law and divine Thought. Cosmic fire and cosmic mind are therefore intimately related throughout *Manvantara*. No form can come into phenomenal existence without the combined action of both.

At the physical level, incandescence and flame constitute a release, and therefore an expression, of the creative fire-mind. The degree of the release is dependent upon the amount of material in which incandescence is physically produced. The extent of the expression of *fohatic* fire, and of the fifth and third Sephiras and their Hosts, is also governed by the size of the fire and the degree of incandescence.

When a fire is kindled, or a match struck, and inflammable substance reduced to ashes, a release occurs on the physical plane of superphysically manifested creative fire. It is this release which acts as an excitant to nature spirits of fire, under which they play and revel exultantly in the physical manifestation of their element.

In order that conjoined cosmic fire and mind may create physical forms, the four other elements of earth, water, air and ether as subtle elements and potencies must also be present, thus completing the five elements essential to the production of natural forms. In physical fire, the subtle element of fire preponderates excessively and is almost exclusively active. Destruction of form, and not construction, is the inevitable result.

CHAPTER III

LIFE AND FORM

THE SIXTH SEPHIRA

THE conjoined Power and Life of the Solar System, manifested as the second Sephira, the solar Lord of Wisdom and all its "sons", find expression as the Life Principle of the material worlds. The One Life of Nature, discrete though it may appear when conceived and viewed from below, is a co-ordinated vehicle for an Intelligence, which is the sixth Sephira. Just as the second Sephira directs the vitalising currents of solar energy at higher levels, so the sixth serves as an expression of the One Life at lower levels including the physical world.

The ocean of the One Life has its shores, which are the physical universe, against which its waves beat continuously in rhythmic pulse. As a beach becomes saturated more and more fully with the rising tides, so physical matter is saturated increasingly with the vitalising fluid, which is the One Life. Evolution for physical substance implies an increase in its vital content, a fuller saturation with the One Life, which is continually conveyed into it by the second and sixth Sephiras.

The first created, solid physical substance is relatively lifeless. In the beginning its life-content is very low. As evolution proceeds, matter gradually becomes increasingly vitalised; component atoms convey and contain greater

148

proportions of Spirit-Life. They then combine more readily
into forms which, in their turn, become proportionately more
responsive to thought. Metaphorically, as the tide rises, the
degree of saturation increases. High watermark represents
the fullest physical manifestation attained in any creative
cycle by Spirit-Life and its embodiments, the first, second
and sixth Sephiras. Saturation point is reached when physical substance becomes most responsive to thought and most
easily moulded by it. Thereafter, the One Mind, as third
and fifth Sephiras, finds in every kind of physical substance
a highly plastic medium in which to fashion the concepts and
products of divine Ideation. All Nature then displays the
most perfect adaptation to universal Thought, whether manifested in Sephirothal Hosts or individualised as man.

Such, in part, is the "work" of the sixth Sephira and its
component Hosts, from Archangels of the solar, vital fluid to
the nature spirit inhabitants and embodiments of the subtle
element of water. In simplest terms, these beings serve as
conductors of *Fohat*, throughout the physical universe, the
"life-blood" of Mother Nature by which she is herself sustained
and by which she nourishes her children.

UNDINES AND SYLPHS—EMANATIONS OF THE SIXTH SEPHIRA

Innumerable "arteries" and "veins" convey throughout
the universe from sun to planets and from planets back to
sun the vital electricity, which is its life-blood. Thus the
sun is the "heart", the universe the "body". Archangels
are interplanetary "transformers" and "transmitters". Angels
are planetary "receivers" and "transmitters", and nature
spirits are the last superphysical recipients of the charge.
This they contain as long as they can and then release or discharge it into the etheric counterpart of Nature. From
there, the physical "beach" or molecular "sands" absorb it

and all Nature is thus vitalised, all substance rendered malleable. The Eternal Oblation is fulfilled.

Intense pleasure is felt by undines and sylphs as they perform their function of recipients and dischargers of solar life.[1] They become filled with ecstasy as they carry out to the limit of their capacity the three functions of absorption of life-force, its retention and compression, and its discharge into their immediate surroundings. This is their life, this their "work", which, as with all nature spirits, is for them but continuous play and, though they do not know it, evolutionary progress is the result. To increase their own joy in this participation in Nature's processes, they try continually to increase their capacity to absorb and retain the vital charge as long as possible. The resultant heightened compression produces an increasingly more powerful, and therefore more joy-producing, discharge.

Evolutionary stature for all the Sephirothal Hosts is measured by their capacity to absorb, contain and compress. As they are thus engaged from dawn to eve of *Manvantara*, their ability to exercise these three functions steadily increases. This, for them, is the way of evolutionary progression, which is marked by an increase both in bodily stature and extension of aura.

The nature spirit, for example, when first it emanates from its parent-angel, may measure but an inch or two in the vertical and horizontal diameters of its aura. The continuing practice throughout vast ages of the absorption, retention and discharge of the electric life of the sun steadily increases the size of both the spherical aura and the once minute, but ever lovely, form within.

THE VISIBLE UNIVERSE

The seventh Sephira is the Lord of all Nature, which is its physical garment. It is immanent throughout this physical

[1] Vide also Part II, Chapter IV, p. 115.

vesture, every atom being created and sustained by the power of which both Sephira and universe are the embodiment and manifestation.

Fohat is the creator. Mind is the designer. Matter is the medium in which creative Spirit fashions the external universe. Not one form in Nature, from atom to similarly spinning planet, comes into existence save as an outcome of the creative Activity of the fire of *Fohat*, the fashioning mind of Spirit, and the receptive, responsive and productive attributes of matter. For this is the eternal, creative Trinity. This is God, the Father, Son and Mother.

The universe is sevenfold. So also must be and are both the active potency and the action of the triple God. Through the agency of the seven Emanations, each the product of a combination of the three supernal Aspects, the Logos "creates" the seven densities which primordial Substance [1] assumes under *fohatic* action and influence. The seventh of these Powers, the seventh Sephira, is a mighty Representative of the Logos at the level of density of the element of earth, and is manifested to the senses of man as atom-built, physical substance. Co-ordination is the predominant power of this Sephira, and the construction and maintenance of physical forms throughout their appropriate time-cycles are its preponderant activity. This task of construction and preservation is fulfilled from within the life-currents of atoms and the forms into which they are built. For therein the deific Presence is enshrined.

The Immanence of God, His indwelling Presence throughout physical Nature, is made manifest as the power, the life and the consciousness of the seventh Sephira. The Transcendence of God is expressed by the remaining Six, each of whom is as the transcendent Logos of the plane immediately below it. Beyond the Seven are Three who constitute the

[1] See paragraph 4, p. 6.

supernal Trinity of the universe. Immanent within these Three, and again transcendent beyond, is that incomprehensible One Alone, which is the first Emanation from the Absolute. Within THAT reside all potencies. From THAT emanate all ideation, power and life. By THAT all worlds are created and sustained. To THAT, in due time according to numerical law, all return.

This One Alone is the Supreme Transcendence, the Primordial Mover "above the surface" of—actually within—pre-cosmic Space. The first "movement" sets going all creative processes, which continue throughout *Manvantara*, just as a pendulum set swinging by a single impulse continues to swing. But the measure of the oscillation and the duration of its continuance depend upon the strength of the initial impulse and the decrees of numerical law. As that agent which imparts to the pendulum that first swing no longer acts, so THAT which imparts to pre-cosmic Substance the first creative impulse no longer acts directly upon the resultant Cosmos. THAT remains, transcendent and alone. Yet from THAT all creation springs; by THAT all creation is moved and lives; in THAT all is contained; to THAT all returns; for, in terms of the outward Cosmos, THAT is infinite and eternal.

The seventh Sephira and its Hosts are the outermost recipients and manifestors of the creative impulse imparted by the One Alone. They represent the extreme limit of the pendulum's swing. Divine Ideation is the core of the being of the seventh Sephira, which is conjoined Spirit-Mind incarnate. According to the archetypal image existent within divine Thought, the seventh Sephira fashions physical Nature. In this process the whole tenfold Sephiroth is involved. All Sephiras converge and are synthesised in the seventh and its form-producing activity. The One Alone, the Sacred Nine and Universal Law contrive to produce that ultimate wonder

of the Cosmos which is physically fashioned divine Ideation,
the material universe.   The seventh Sephira, who is the tenth
if the supernal Three be included, is a synthesis of all, as also
is its outer garb, the natural world; for the conjoined whole
of the Powers is contained within atom, molecule and form of
the physical plane.

THE ARCHETYPE

Nature's varied forms have their origin in Universal
Mind, which is the third expression of the manifested One,
as Will and Life are the first and second.   The idea of every
form arises spontaneously within Universal Mind, as a manifestation under numerical law of that portion of Cosmic
Ideation which is to be expressed within a single universe.
In origin and "seed", all forms are one.   That one form may
be mentally—and therefore imperfectly and incompletely—
conceived as a point within a sphere.   The point is the germ.
The sphere is the egg.   From these two, creative centre and
circumscribed region, the universe evolves.

Multiplicity of form arises from the single germ or Archetype, as creative Will and Life move outwards from the centre
into the field.   The potentialities within the germ then begin
to become actualities.   The latent combinations and permu-
tations of the several components of the germ, each expressive
of universal Ideation, become operative influences, as divine
Thought seeks external expression as form.

The "still" thought of the universe is in essence single;
its active thought is multiple.   The timeless, changeless Archetype, whilst containing the potentiality of all forms, is itself
a single "creation" or projection from divine Ideation.   As
its vibrating energies, or "chords", impinge upon the external,
enclosing matter, mental forms arise therein.   These forms
are gradually densified and at the same time diversified.   At
the physical level the extreme of both density and diversity

is attained. Nature there displays her greatest variety as thought after thought of the divine Mind becomes manifest. Thus the One becomes the many, which arise from within the One.

THE FAIRY BUILDERS OF FORM

The ultimate fashioners of form are the nature spirits of the element of earth—gnome and brownie—assisted by those of air—fairy and sylph. Unconsciously they aid the designer, Universal Thought, by playing in the fields of force set up by the impact of creative energy as "sound" upon responsive, fructified matter. This establishment of fields of force of varied geometrical designs occurs, not in dense substance, but in the ether which is both mould and matrix of all forms, Mother Nature's womb. Pleasure is gained by nature spirits in moving, dancing and flying along the lines of force within the fields. This fairy motion accentuates these lines in the ether, as does a pencil line drawn again and again on paper.

All elements meet at the physical level. All nature spirits participate through play and movement along the lines of force, save those of fire who are associated with the currents of creative energy by which the fields of force are set up. Gnome and brownie, fairy and sylph, unconsciously play their part in the slow production of Nature's forms in etheric and solid matter. The aerial hosts begin the work. Gnomes, brownies and the like within the earth ultimately fashion the purely solid, densest forms.

The secret of these workers in mineral, metal, jewel and organic forms, is Nature's own and may not be revealed to man, it is said, outside her Sanctuaries, and there only to those who first have willingly lent themselves to the Goddess as co-workers in her "quarries" without thought or hope of reward. The apprentice master-builder learns very gradually, and by experiment, these thaumaturgic secrets of the creation

of forms by Will-Thought in co-operation with the Sephirothal
Hosts.   They can no more be conveyed in words alone than
can the secrets of success in any art.   They must be discovered,
or arise within the craftsman's mind as he experiments.

The little workmen are everywhere and ceaselessly at
work.   No smallest form of any kind appears unassociated
with a builder of form, in none of whom can a thought of self
arise.   Individuality is not born in them.   Inwardly moved
by the action within them of Universal Thought, which is
their Mother Source, and of their sephirothal senior, their
life is one of thought-free, spontaneous play within and with
the currents of creative energy flowing through them and
their subtle element.

CHAPTER IV

THE SEPHIROTHAL TREE

THE Kabbalah has been variously described as an unwritten or oral tradition, as the esoteric doctrine of the Jewish religion and as the hidden wisdom or theosophy of the Hebrew Rabbis of the Middle Ages, who obtained it from the older secret doctrines concerning divine truths and cosmogony.

The Hebrew word is derived from the root QBL, "to receive". Included in the meaning of the word, therefore, is the practice of transmitting esoteric knowledge by word of mouth. On examination, the Kabbalah proves to be a system of theosophy which claims to be of celestial origin and to have reached the early Hebrew patriarchs through the ministry of the angels. King David and King Solomon are said to have been initiated into the Kabbalah, and Rabbi Simeon Ben Jochai daringly took the step of writing a portion of the teachings down at the time of the destruction of the second Temple. His son, Rabbi Eleazar, his secretary and his disciples gathered together his treatises and from them composed the *Zohar*, meaning "Splendour", which is the literary source of Kabbalism.

THE TEN ORDERS OF ANGELS

The Angelic Hosts occupy an important place in the cosmogonical scheme of the Kabbalah. Ten Orders are associated with the ten Sephiras, which constitute the kabbalistic Tree of Life. They are regarded as Emanations of Deity, each Sephira representing a number, a group of exalted ideas, titles and attributes, and a hierarchy of spiritual beings outside of humanity. Each Sephira has a fourfold nature according to its association with each of the four worlds of the Kabbalist. These are: "Atziluth", the Archetypal World, or World of Emanations, the Divine World; "Briah", the World of Creation, also called Khorsis, the World of Thrones; "Yetzirah", the World of Formation and of Angels; "Assiah", the World of Action, the World of Matter.

In Atziluth, the Sephiras manifest through ten different aspects represented by the ten holy names of God in the Hebrew Scriptures. In Briah, the Sephiras manifest through the ten Archangels. In Yetzirah, they manifest through the Choirs or Hosts of the Angels. In Assiah, and especially on the physical plane, they are associated with the physical planets and the subtle elements of which they are said to be composed. By correspondence they are also associated with the *chakras* in the etheric double of man and their related glandular and nerve centres.

The Sephiras are also depicted as circles. As Proclus says: "Before the mathematical numbers, there are the *self-moving* numbers; before the figures apparent, the vital figures, and before producing the material worlds *which move in a circle*, the Creative Power produced the invisible circles." [1] At the head of each hierarchy of spiritual Intelligences is a named Archangel, under whom are gradations of angels who perform significant functions in the emanation, formation, preservation and transformation of a universe.

The Christian religion, which contains much kabbalistic thought, teaches that there are nine Orders of angels called, severally, Angels and Archangels, Thrones, Dominations, Principalities, Virtues, Powers, Cherubim and Seraphim.

---

[1] Quoted in *The Secret Doctrine*, Vol. IV, p. 122, Adyar Edition.

Certain qualities and activities are assigned to each of these Orders. Angels and Archangels are sent as messengers in matters of high importance, as were Gabriel and Raphael. Thrones contemplate the glory and equity of the divine judgments and teach men to rule with justice. Dominations are supposed to regulate the activities and duties of the angels. Principalities preside over peoples and provinces and serve as angelic rulers of the nations of the world. Virtues have the gift of working miracles. Powers are a check on evil spirits. Cherubim excel in the splendour of knowledge and so enlighten mankind with wisdom; and the Seraphim, being most ardent in divine love, inspire mankind with that quality. In nearly all the Biblical accounts of men's visions of God, He is described as transcendent in glory and surrounded by countless multitudes of His angels.

Kabbalism, whilst naming them differently, gives to these beings their due place and certain additional functions. In common with other cosmogonies, it postulates the existence of an Absolute as the basis of everything. This is regarded as negative existence or no-thing and has been described as an illimitable abyss of glory. This negative existence has three veils which are called AIN, meaning the negatively existent, AIN SOPH, the limitless without form, being or likeness with anything else, and AIN SOPH AUR, the limitless light which concentrates into the first and highest Sephira of the Sephirothal Tree called Kether, the Crown. The nine [1] letters AIN SOPH AUR are said to shadow forth the nine Sephiras as hidden ideas or seed-thoughts which, when manifestation begins, are represented by archangelic Beings or Gods. In the description of this process, the Limitless Ocean of Light is said to concentrate a centre, which is the first Sephira, the Crown, which in turn gives birth to the nine others, the last or tenth being called Malkuth, the Kingdom, meaning "all Nature

[1] PH (as in SOPH)—P in the Hebrew alphabet.

THE SEPHIROTHAL TREE
ACCORDING TO THE KABBALAH

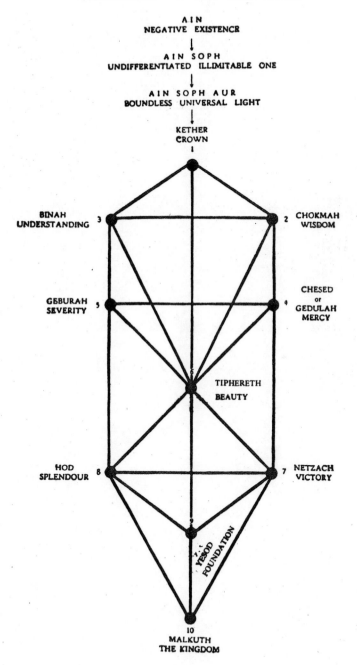

AIN
NEGATIVE EXISTENCE

AIN SOPH
UNDIFFERENTIATED ILLIMITABLE ONE

AIN SOPH AUR
BOUNDLESS UNIVERSAL LIGHT

KETHER
CROWN
1

BINAH
UNDERSTANDING 3

CHOKMAH
WISDOM 2

GEBURAH
SEVERITY 5

CHESED
or
GEDULAH
MERCY 4

6 TIPHERETH
BEAUTY

HOD
SPLENDOUR 8

7 NETZACH
VICTORY

9 YESOD
FOUNDATION

10
MALKUTH
THE KINGDOM

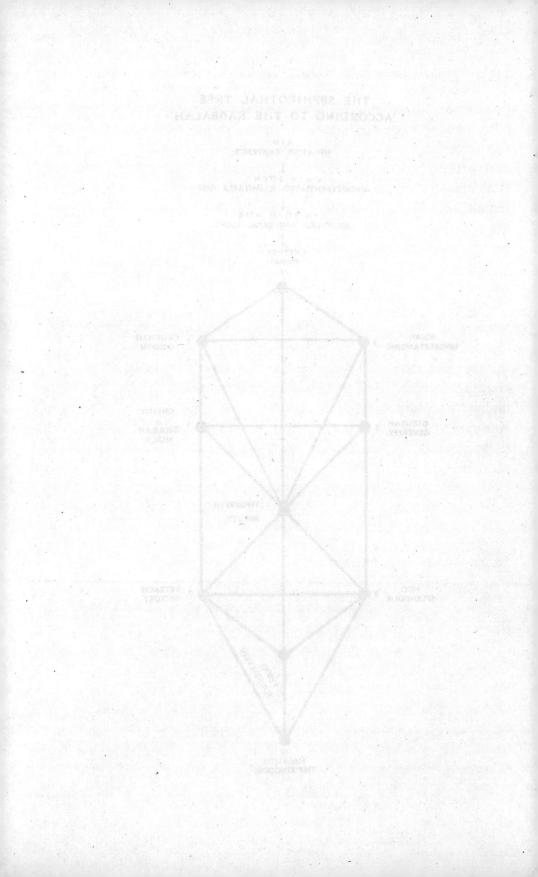

manifested". Together, the ten Sephiras represent the emanation and development of the powers and attributes of Deity. Each number is an outward symbol for inner creative forces and processes and their personifications as Archangels or Builders of the universe. Some of these are male and some female, or rather of positive and negative potencies, Deity having conformed Itself thus in order that It could create. Man, being made in the image of Deity, is male and female also.

KETHER

The first Sephira is Number One, the Monad of Pythagoras. As already stated, this Sephira is called Kether, the Crown, and also the Ancient of the Ancient Ones, the Ancient of Days, the Primordial Point, the White Head, the Inscrutable Height and the Vast Countenance or Macroposopus. In its highest and abstract aspect it is in association with Adam Kadmon (the Heavenly Man)—a collective name—who is a synthesis of the whole Sephirothal Tree, the Archetype of all creation and all humanity, and the first Adam of Genesis. He is also called *Seir Anpin*, "Son of the Concealed Father", and so in this highest aspect must be regarded as the Logos, the Christos of the Fourth Gospel.

Since one cannot create alone, Kether is said to vibrate across the field of manifestation or to reflect itself in matter to produce a feminine or dyad, from which in turn all creation and all beings emanate, having been hitherto contained within Kether. The Archangel Head of the associated hierarchy of angels is severally named Metatron, Prince of Faces or "beside (or beyond) the Throne", Angel of the Presence, World Prince, El Shaddai, the Omnipotent and Almighty One, the Messenger and Shekinah, also associated with the cloud of glory which rested on the Mercy Seat upon the Ark of the Covenant,[1] within the Holy of Holies. Shekinah is

[1] *Exodus*, XL. 35.

also regarded as identical with AIN SOPH AUR, the veil of AIN SOPH, pre-cosmic Substance or virgin Space, the *Mulaprakriti* or *Parabrahmic* root of Hinduism.

The Order of angels is the Chaioth Ha-Qadesh, "Holy Living Creatures". They are associated with the Kerubim,[1] are pictured as sphinxes and regarded as Governors of the four elements in their highest sublimation. They would seem to correspond to the *Lipika*, the Celestial Recorders or "Scribes", the Agents of *Karma* of Hinduism. The hierarchy is concerned with the initiation of the whirling motions by means of which primordial atoms or "holes in space" are formed, presumably using the force which in Tibetan is called *Fohat*, the essence of cosmic electricity, the ever-present electrical energy and ceaseless formative and destructive power in the universe, the universal propelling, vital force, the *primum mobile*, whose symbol is the *svastika*. In Kether are thus said to be the "beginnings of the whirls", the first stirrings of the divine creative Essence. One of the chief duties of the members of this Angelic Hierarchy is to receive this Essence in Kether and carry it to the succeeding hierarchy of the Auphanim or "Wheels", associated with the second Sephira.

CHOKMAH

Kether produces the other nine Sephiras, the second being Chokmah, Wisdom, a masculine active potency or Father reflected from Kether. Chokmah is the second Adam, from whom is produced Eve, and is associated with Microposopus, the Lesser Countenance. The Archangel Head of the Angelic Hierarchy is Ratziel, "the Herald of Deity", "the Delight of God". The Order of angels is the Auphanim or "Wheels", so-called in reference to the vortex, whirlwind or whirlpool-producing action of the *primum mobile*. From

---

[1] Usually spelt in Kabbalism with a " K " rather than " Ch " and so pronounced.

this Order are said to be drawn the Angels of the Planets, who are described in the First Chapter of *Ezekiel*. The planetary correspondence is with the Zodiac and, in some systems, Uranus.

BINAH

The third Sephira is a feminine, passive potency called Binah, Intelligence, the Understanding, co-equal and contemporaneous with Chokmah, to whom she is as Eve, the Mother Supernal. Binah is also called Ama, Eternal, combined with Ab, Father, for the maintenance of the universe in order. She is sometimes called the Great Sea and, kabbalistically, these two Powers weave the web of the universe. The Archangel Head is Tzaphqiel, "He who beholds God", or "Contemplation of God". The Order of angels is the Arelim, "the Mighty Ones", the Thrones of Christian angelology. The number Two as a principle is like two straight lines which can never enclose a space, and is therefore powerless till number Three forms a primary triangle. This Binah does, and makes evident the supernal, but not the material, active Trinity. This upper Triad remains in the Archetypal World, whilst the seven Sephiras which follow create, sustain and transform the manifested, material World. The planet associated with Binah is Saturn.

The union of Chokmah and Binah, Wisdom and Understanding, produces Supernal Knowledge, called Daath in Kabbalism. Daath itself is not regarded as a Sephira, but is included in some diagrams of the Sephirothal Tree, in which it is placed between Chokmah and Binah.

CHESED

An active dyad now exists in Chokmah and Binah. Their union produced Chesed, a masculine or active potency. Chesed is Mercy or Love and is also called Gedulah,

Greatness or Magnificence. The Archangel Head is Tzadqiel, "Justice of God", "Righteousness of God". The Order of angels is the Chasmalim or "Scintillating Flames", or "Brilliant Ones". They are the Dominations of Christian angelology and are regarded as angels of light. The planet is Jupiter.

GEBURAH

From Four or Chesed emanated the feminine, passive, fifth potency, Geburah, Severity, Strength, Fortitude, Justice. This Sephira is also called Pachad, Fear. The Archangel Head is Khamael, "the Right Hand of God", and is sometimes called the Punishing Angel. The Order of angels is the Seraphim, known in Christian angelology as Powers. They are thus described in *Isaiah* VI. 1-3:

"I saw also the Lord sitting upon a throne, high and lifted up, and his train filled the temple.

"Above it stood the seraphims: each one had six wings; with twain he covered his face, and with twain he covered his feet, and with twain he did fly.

"And one cried unto another, and said, Holy, holy, holy, is the Lord of hosts: the whole earth is full of his glory."

The Hebrew name of the Seraphim is translated "Serpents", and as this is related to the verbal root ShRP, "to burn up", it may be assumed that these are the fiery Serpents associated with the creative fire and processes in both Nature and man. The planet is Mars.

TIPHERETH

From Chesed (masculine) and Geburah (feminine) emanated the sixth and uniting Sephira, Tiphereth, Beauty or Mildness, the heart and centre of the Sephirothal Tree. This is said to be the place allotted by the Israelites to the Messiah and by the early Christians to the Christ. The Archangel

Head is Michael, "who is like unto God". The Order of angels is the Malachim, meaning "Kings" and known in Christianity as Virtues. Another system places Raphael here, and Michael in the eighth Sephira. The "planet" is the Sun.

In terms of planes of Nature and levels of normal human consciousness, Tiphereth marks both a boundary and a place of union between the Divine and the human, the Macrocosm and the microcosm, the Abstract and the concrete. Here is said to exist, symbolically, Paroketh, the so-called Veil of the temple both of seven-planed Nature and of seven-principled man. This Veil must be pierced by those who would ascend in consciousness the middle pillar of the Tree of Life, liberate themselves from the purely human delusion of separated self-hood which must be "crucified" and enter into realisation of unity with the One Great Self of All. Thereafter the occult forces of the abstract or formless worlds and their angelic directors may be invoked both to quicken human evolution by arousing the hidden forces in the force-centres in the personal nature and body of man and to assist in various kinds of occult work.

By the union of Geburah or Severity, Justice and Chesed or Mercy, Beauty, Harmony, Clemency are produced, and the second Sephirothal Trinity is complete. This sixth Sephira, Tiphereth, with the fourth, fifth, seventh, eighth and ninth, is spoken of as the Microposopus or Lesser Countenance, the reflection into manifestation of Macroposopus, and its antithesis.

NETZACH

The seventh Sephira is Netzach, Firmness, Victory. The Archangelic Head is called Hamiel, "the Grace of God", and the Order of angels is the Elohim, "the Gods", also called Tsarshisim, "Brilliant Ones", known as Principalities in

Christianity. Hamiel, it is, who is said to be thus described in the *Book of Daniel*, Chapter X. 5, 6:

" Then I lifted up mine eyes, and looked, and behold a certain man clothed in linen, whose loins were girded with fine gold of Uphaz:

" His body also was like the beryl and his face as the appearance of lightning, and his eyes as lamps of fire, and his arms and his feet like in colour to polished brass, and the voice of his words like the voice of a multitude."

The planet associated with this Sephira is Venus.

HOD

From Netzach proceeded the feminine, passive potency, Hod, the eighth Sephira, Splendour, the God of Armies. The Archangel Head is Raphael, "Divine Physician", the Angel of Healing, intermediary between man and God, who is assisted by a hierarchy of ministering angels known in one interpretation as the Beni Elohim, "the Sons of God", and as Archangels in Christianity. The planet is Mercury.

YESOD

Hod and Netzach together produced the ninth Sephira. Yesod, the Foundation of Basis, "the Mighty Living One". The Archangel Head is Gabriel, "the Mighty One of God". The Order of angels is the Kerubim, "the Holy Living Creatures", the Angels of Christianity. Evidently an intimate connection exists between the Kerubim of the first Sephira in the supernal worlds and those of Yesod in the etheric counterpart and body of the outer, material universe. They are sometimes called Aishim or "the Flames" and are also referred to as the four angels of the subtle elements of earth, fire, water and air.

The Kerubim are associated with the constellations of Taurus, Leo, Scorpio and Aquarius, or the Bull, the Lion, the Eagle and the Man. Part of their duty is said to be to gather the forces of Nature on the astral plane and pour them into the Kingdom of Earth, Malkuth, and to control them in all their complex manifestations. They are also regarded as agents of the *Lipika* or Recorders, the Lords of *Karma* and Regents of the four quarters of the universe. The planet is the Moon. Netzach, Hod and Yesod together complete the third Trinity in the Sephirothal Tree.

MALKUTH

From the ninth Sephira came the tenth and last, completing the decade of the numbers. It is called Malkuth, the Kingdom of Earth, all Nature, and also the Queen, Matrona, the Inferior Mother. Malkuth is sometimes called Shekinah and so would seem to represent the veil both of primordial Matter and of physical Nature.

Two Archangels are associated with Malkuth. They are the Metatron of Kether and his brother and co-worker, Sandalphon, the kabbalistic Prince of Angels. Sandalphon, the Dark Angel, may be regarded as the densely material *shakti* or power of Metatron, the Bright Angel. Since the physical plane of the planet Earth is the place of the outworking of man's physical *karma*, Sandalphon is sometimes regarded as an Angel of personal *karma*. Metatron, on the other hand, is associated with the Celestial Agents of *Karma* who are concerned with the *karma* of the human race as a whole. The Archangel of our Earth in particular is said to be Auriel, "the Light of God". The Order of angels is the Ishim or "Fires". No single planet, unless it be the Earth, is allotted to Malkuth, which apparently includes the whole of physical Nature and is concerned with the four subtle and material elements and their use in the building and transformation of the "kingdom" of the visible universe.

THE TREE OF LIFE IN MAN

Such, in part, is the Tree of Life of the Kabbalah, said to be derived from the primeval Secret Doctrine of the East.

It is regarded as one of the great master symbols and keys of occult science. With the Hebrew alphabet, it is said to exemplify the principle that evolution is simple or single at the source, and infinitely complex in manifestation.

This mathematical diagram sets forth a system by which man can rise to spiritual heights by manifesting in and through himself the qualities of the ten Sephiras. As he awakens in himself his inherent powers, represented in the universe by each of the ten Sephiras, and in himself physically by his nerve and glandular centres and superphysically by his *chakras* and their vivifying triune Serpent Fire, he enters into conscious *rapport* with the Orders of angels associated with each, and ultimately with their Archangelic Heads. Thus attuned, he collaborates with them and they with him, in the fulfilment of the Great Work [1] to which both angels and men are called.

In every man, indeed, exist potentially *Rashith Ha-Galgalim*, the *primum mobile*, the beginning of whirling motions of Kether; the *Masloth*, the sphere of the Zodiac, of Chokmah; the *Shabbathai* or rest, Saturn of Binah; the *Tzedeq*, righteousness, Jupiter of Chesed; the *Madim*, vehement strength, Mars of Geburah; the *Shemesh*, the solar light, the Sun of Tiphereth; the *Nogah*, glittering splendour, Venus of Netzach; the *Kokab*, the stellar light, Mercury of Hod; the *Levanah*, the lunar flame, the Moon of Yesod; the *Cholom Yesodoth*, the breaker of the foundations, the elements of Malkuth. All these exist potentially within every man, and throughout his existence he gradually unfolds the whole pattern and image of Deity which ultimately is made manifest in him. Then he fulfils his destiny as enunciated by Our

---

[1] A term from the Ancient Mysteries denoting the process of the creation, preservation and transformation to perfection of the universe and man. Microcosmically, it is the emancipation of the human will, the full development and conquest of all man's faculties and the transmutation of all that is gross into that which is pure. In material alchemy the Great Work includes the separation of the subtle from the gross and the transmutation of base metals into gold. Mystically, the Great Work consists of a corresponding interior achievement by which the glory of the spiritual light is obtained and all darkness is dispelled for ever. Vide *Transcendental Magic*, E. Levi. Chapter XII.

THE AURIC TREE OF LIFE

THE AURIC TREE OF LIFE
ATZILUTH

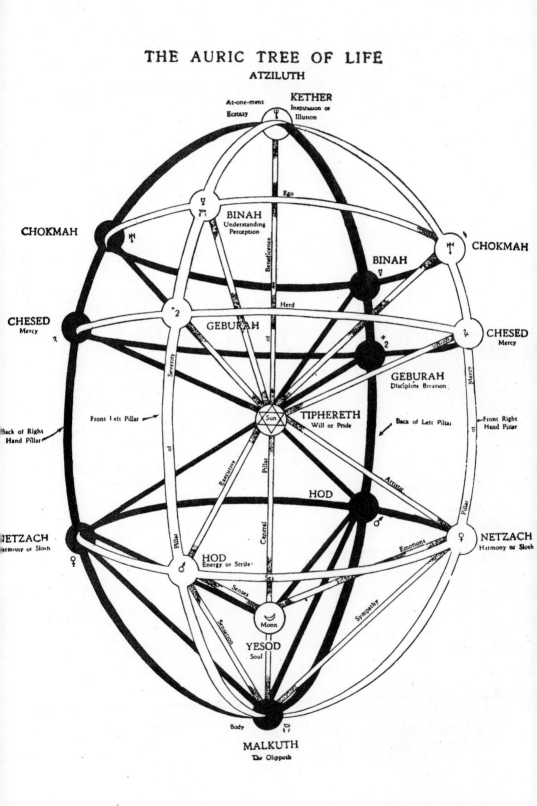

KETHER

At-one-ment
Ecstasy

Inspiration or
Illusion

Ego

CHOKMAH

BINAH
Understanding
Perception

BINAH

CHOKMAH

Beneficence

Herd

CHESED
Mercy

GEBURAH

CHESED
Mercy

GEBURAH
Discipline Bisvation

Severity

Front Left Pillar

Back of Right
Hand Pillar

TIPHERETH
Will or Pride

Sun

Back of Left Pillar

Front Right
Hand Pillar

Mercy

Executive

Pillar

Artistic

HOD

NETZACH
Harmony or Sloth

HOD
Energy or Strife

Central

Pillar

Emotions

NETZACH
Harmony or Sloth

Senses

Sympathy

Moon

YESOD
Soul

Body

MALKUTH
The Qlippoth

Lord: "Ye shall be perfect, even as your Father which is in heaven is perfect",[1] and completes, as far as he himself is concerned, the Great Work.

THE AURIC TREE OF LIFE

In the diagram, the Auric Tree of Life, an attempt is made to portray the microcosmic tree as it presumably exists in man. This diagram shows the areas in the subtle bodies which are vibrating in unison with the Regents of the planets and the Zodiacal Signs, each of whom have their representations in the nature, the aura and the physical body of man, thereby linking Macrocosm with microcosm.

The middle pillar of the diagram corresponds to the spinal cord and the feminine column containing Binah, Geburah and Hod would be on the right side, and the masculine pillar containing Chokmah, Chesed and Netzach on the left. These three currents of force may also refer to the three-fold creative Serpent Fire in Nature and in man with its triple currents and their channels called *Ida* (feminine), *Pingala* (masculine) and *Sushumna* (neutral and spinal).

If the two currents of force represented by the two pillars (white in the diagram) in the front of the aura are followed over the head, where they will presumably cross, then they will travel down the back of the aura (black in the diagram) on opposite sides to make four pillars in all, with the central one in the midst.

In practical, esoteric Kabbalism these forces, *chakras* and correspondences with the Creative Intelligences of the universe are aroused into conscious activity by means of various forms of meditation, ritual invocations to the Gods who are addressed by their Divine Names and other *mantric* titles, magical ceremonials and very potent prayers. This Chapter closes with one version of an ancient kabbalistic prayer.

[1] *Matthew* V. 48. RV.

Universal God, One Light, One Life, One Power,
Thou All in All, beyond expression, beyond comprehension,
Oh, Nature! Thou something from No-thing,
Thou symbol of Wisdom,
In myself I am nothing,
In Thee I am I.
I live in Thee,
Live Thou in me,
And bring me out of the region of self,
Into the eternal Light.

AMEN

CHAPTER V

THE INVERSE SEPHIRAS
AND THE PROBLEM OF EVIL

SATAN AND ARMAGEDDON

IN occult philosophy, Deity is Eternal Life, manifested in form according to numerical law in *Manvantara* and unmanifest in any form conceivable by the human mind in *Pralaya*. In one aspect, Satan is Eternal Substance, resistingly shaped into forms by the One Life during *Manvantara*, and remaining formless during *Pralaya*.

The Archangels and angels in their ten Orders make manifest Eternal Life according to the "Word". In one of their many aspects, the Inverse Sephiras are expressions of Eternal Substance and its inherent spirit of resistance to Life. In man these two meet, and his Herculean task is to bring them to perfect equipoise. As Adept, he achieves this in his own nature. As Logos, he establishes it in a Solar System of his own emanation. Since man is the only being in whom spirit and matter are equally present, he becomes the battle-ground of the universe. Armageddon is waged within him. The spirit in him suffers continual "defeat" until the day of the development of the Higher Mind. From that time onwards, the "defeat" of matter is assured. When the light of intuition begins to shine within man, victory is in his hands. As a race he then establishes brotherhood on his planetary home. As an individual he "enters the Stream", becoming an Initiate of the Greater Mysteries, and later an Adept.[1]

As manifested powers, both spirit and matter are septenates, and find expression in and through seven principles. Those of Deity are the modifications in Divine consciousness of which the seven states of matter are the material product. The seven principles of Satan, in the occult sense, are those seven planes of matter and their seven sub-planes. Neither Satan as a personal devil, an isolated embodiment of infamy, nor God as an extra-Cosmic, almighty, infinite yet personal, moral Governor, whose laws can be abrogated or modified by personal persuasion or bargaining, as assumed in the popular imagination or the theological mind, has any place in occult philosophy. There is truth in the concept of a Cosmic pair of opposites, spirit and matter, activity and inertia, construction and destruction, I-am-ness and I-am-all-ness, but their man-made images are a delusion.

Nevertheless, in their exoteric aspects, almost all religions have promulgated the idea of an Evil Being in perpetual opposition to the Supreme Deity. Popular Christianity is no exception, though, as is the case with so many of its doctrines, the Satanic form has changed with the passage of time. Dante described the Devil as a giant with three heads, coloured red, yellow and black. Milton and Goethe presented a tragic, yet heroic and even reasonable, man of the world. The Devil has also been made to wear a one-piece suit of red and to be armed with a pitchfork. Behind these popular images is a concept of Satan as a fallen angel, a once-pure spirit, continually tempting man to sin. Since evil is a negative quality, being merely the lack of good in man, and Satan is the embodiment of that evil, he cannot be regarded as a positive, existing principle. Rather does he represent the absence of the good, empty spaces in the omnipresent web of the universe,

[1] Vide *Initiation and the Perfecting of Man*, Annie Besant, T.P.H., Adyar.

interstices, perhaps, in the warp and weft upon which the great Weaver perpetually weaves, or manifests outwardly, Divine ideas.

The existence of both Devil and evil is intimately associated with the attribute of free-will in man. Within the structure of cosmic law, and apart from the irresistible evolutionary thrust, man possesses the freedom to think, plan, speak and act either in accordance with Nature's purpose or against it. When, whether consciously or unconsciously, he operates against it, he becomes an antagonist of cosmic purpose. In consequence, he generates for himself adverse or "evil" experiences and conditions of life. If he continues, he tends to become cut off from the currents of the universal Life-force, isolated, a being of death rather than of life. Some men have thus continued to exercise their freedom of action. They are the so-called black magicians, the Dark Powers, the followers of the Left Hand Path, the Lords of the Dark Face, the dread Brothers of the Shadow. Their destiny is not to be annihilated, but to sink into the condition known as *Avichi*, the "wave-less", the opposite pole to Nirvana to which the Adepts of the Right Hand Path attain. Ultimately, in a later cycle of manifestation, these who become highly developed embodiments of self-separateness re-embark upon the involutionary and evolutionary journey. Satan himself, if regarded as an existent being, would seem to have exercised this freedom; for at some time he must have chosen a path of individualistic, self-separative motive and action.

Thus, in one aspect, Satan is a personification of *Ahamkara*, the I-making impulse from which arises the delusion of self-separateness within omnipresent Spirit-Life. All evil, and in consequence all human sorrow, is said to spring from this heresy of "separateness". In another aspect, the fabulous monster which is the Satan of popular theology may be regarded as an excuse, a scapegoat, someone to take the blame for the errors into which humanity falls whilst passing through the purely emotional and mental (especially) phases of its evolution.

The action of the Inverse Sephira, Beelzebub, " God of Flies ", Prince of Devils,[1] may be taken as an example of the place granted in occult philosophy to some of the dark Numerations. They are regarded in general as personifications of the resistance of matter to the harmonising process which Nature must achieve in and through her son—man—before the close of *Maha-Manvantara*. This resistance cannot with truth be regarded as evil, since without it there could be no development and expression of latent powers.

As the scarab beetle encloses the seed of its life in a ball of mud, so, it would seem, does Beelzebub, also named Lord of Scarabs, enshroud the Monads of men in material vehicles. Having performed its enclosing function, the scarab rolls the ball of mud to a sunny spot and leaves it to its own devices and to the influence of the sun. Ultimately the egg hatches and brings forth the larva which becomes the winged scarab, in its turn parent of further eggs. Beelzebub, in its esoteric meaning, may perhaps be regarded as a personification of that impulse, which the scarab shares with all Nature, to enclose life in forms, Monads in bodies, and to send them forth on their cyclic journeyings or bind them to the wheel of major and minor cycles. That is probably why the scarab was sacred in Egypt; for as an insect, it habitually exhibits one of Nature's most mysterious powers and attributes.

One Order of the Inverse Sephiras, possibly the second and third Numerations, are Intelligences who fashioned the mental, emotional and etheric-physical bodies of the first three Races of men to inhabit this earth in this world period. These *Pitris*, as they are called in Hinduism, also fulfilled the office of " inducting " or " luring " the Monad-Egos of those

[1] *Matthew* X, 25.

Races into the bodies which they had constructed for them. Since this materialising function appears evil from the point of view of the evolutionary arc which tends towards spiritualisation, these Intelligences are sometimes referred to as the Satanic Hierarchies. As is stated in Part V, "The Miracle of Birth and the World Mother", when investigating the descent of human Egos into birth, I received evidence that a corresponding function is still performed by members of the Angelic Hosts for all human beings on the pre-natal or downward " arc " of the cycle of each successive birth, when the Ego projects a ray of its power, life and consciousness from the realm of Spiritual Intelligence in which it abides. Members of one Order of the Angelic Hosts assist in building the mental, emotional, etheric-physical bodies, in their mutual adjustment and in the induction of human consciousness into them.

Whilst the enshrouding, burying, embodying function of certain of the Inverse Sephiras does impose temporary limitations upon the life within, it cannot truly be regarded as evil. Neither can the Intelligences concerned with these processes, be regarded, with any truth, as Satanic; for descent is essential to ascent, temporary embodiment to the development of latent powers. In the Egyptian religion, the God " Khepera, ' he who rolls ', was the ' father ' of the Gods and the creator of all things in heaven and earth . . . self-begotten and self-born . . . identified with the rising sun and new birth generally." [1]

In Kabbalism, the Inverse Sephiras are opposite Numerations to the Superior Sephiras. They are personifications of functions apparently opposed to those which the Superior Sephiras perform. The former are on the side of matter and the latter on that of spirit. The former accentuate the *guna* [2]

[1] *The Gods of Egypt,* Budge.

[2] *guna*, Sanskrit. The three divisions of the inherent qualities of differentiated matter, *Rajas*, activity and desire; *sattva*, balance and pure quiescence; *tamas*, inertia, stagnation,

of *tamas*, the latter *rajas*. The middle pillar in the diagram of the Sephirothal Tree represents, in one aspect, man the harmoniser, the balancer, the embodied principle of equilibrium. His office in the universe is to establish and maintain *sattva*.

The symbol of involution, the blazing sword with curved blade, resembling a lightning flash, is portrayed in the Tree of Life by means of a line drawn from Kether through Chokmah, Binah, Chesed, Geburah, Tiphereth, Netzach, Hod and Yesod into Malkuth. The evolutionary path, symbolised by the caduceus, the wand of Hermes, in one of its many meanings, is obtained by two lines rising from Malkuth, proceeding upwards and crossing over at each Sephira of the central pillar.

THE ARCH-FIENDS

The Inverse Sephiras in their ten degrees thus answer to the decade of the Sephiroth, but in inverse ratio, as darkness and impurity increase with the descent of each degree.[1] This position becomes apparent when the functions of the Inverse Sephiras are compared with those of their corresponding Superior Sephiras. The former are also referred to as the Lords of Unbalanced Forces, sometimes associated with " the Kings that reigned in the land of Edom, before there reigned any king over the children of Israel ".[2] Kabbalistically they are linked with the Qliphoth who were Intelligences or *Pitris* connected with the deepest phases of the process of involution or forthgoing at which, before the path of return was entered upon, a condition of unbalance or non-equilibrium between spirit and matter existed for a time. In terms of human evolution the kings of Edom referred to the Archetypal, shadowy,

and decay. These correspond to the three aspects of the various Trinities, Brahma, Vishnu and Shiva respectively.

[1] Vide *The Kabbalah Unveiled*, S. L. MacGregor Mathers, p. 30.

[2] *Genesis* XXXVI, 31.

non-physical, "pre-Adamite" first race of men on earth which was androgynous or created before the balance of the sexes. The equilibrated compound of spirit and matter, positive and negative, male and female came about after the separation of the sexes in the later Third Root Race.

The Orders of retrograde spirits and Arch-fiends correspond to the angels and Archangels, and are enumerated by A. E. Waite in his book *The Doctrine and Literature of the Kabalah* as follows:

" I.   THAUMIEL, the doubles of God, said to be two-headed and so named, because they pretend to be equal to the Supreme Crown. This is properly the title of the averse *Sephira* corresponding to *Kether*. The cortex is CATHARIEL, according to the Supplements of the Zohar. Satan and Moloch are said to be the arch-demons, but the attributions are hopelessly confused throughout, partly owing to the obscure classifications of the Zohar and the contradictions of later Kabalists.

" II.   CHAIGIDIEL, a term connecting with the significance of *placenta*, or, according to other authorities, with that of obstruction, in the sense of an impediment to the heavenly influx. This averse *Sephira* corresponds to *Chokmah*. Its cortices are the OGHIEL or GHOGIEL which cleave to illusory or material appearances in opposition to those of reality and wisdom. This explanation is, of course, very late. The arch-demon is said to be ADAM BELIAL, and so again is Beelzebuth. The Dukes of Esau are also connected with this number.

" III.   SATHARIEL, the concealment of God, meaning that this averse *Sephira*, unlike *Binah*, or Intelligence, hides the face of mercy. In the Supplements of the Zohar it is termed SHEIRIEL, from the hirsute body of Esau. The Dukes of Esau are referred to this number, instead of to the averse correspondence of *Chokmah*, by the same work. LUCIFUGE is said to be the arch-demon, but this is obviously not a Kabalistic term; it is known, however, to the grimories and to some later demonologists of the Latin church.

" IV. GAMCHICOTH, or GOG SHEKLAH, disturber of all things, the averse correspondence of *Chesed*. According to the Zoharic Supplements the cortex seems to be AZARIEL. The arch-demon is ASTAROTH in late Kabalism.

" V. GOLAB, or burning in the sense of incendiarism. This is the averse correspondence of *Geburah* and the antithesis of the Seraphim or Fiery Serpents. The cortex is USIEL. The arch-demon of late Kabalism is ASMODEUS.

" VI. TOGARINI, wranglers, because, according to Isaac de Loria, this averse correspondence of *Tiphereth* strives with the supernal *Geburah*. The cortices are called ZOMIEL and the arch-demon is BELAHEGOR.

" VII. HARAB SERAP, dispersing raven, referring to the idea that this bird drives out its young, the averse correspondence of *Netzach*. The cortices are the THEUMIEL and the arch-demon is BAAL CHANAN.

" VIII. SAMAEL, or embroilment, corresponding to *Hod*, the supernal Victory. The cortices are THEUNIEL according to the Supplements of the Zohar, and ADRAMALEK is the name assigned to the arch-demon by late writers.

" IX.   GAMALIEL, the obscene, in averse correspondence
with *Jesod*, which signifies the generation of the
higher order.   OGIEL, which other classifications
attribute to the averse correspondence of *Chesed*,
seems to be the cortex mentioned in the Zoharic
Supplements, and the arch-fiend is LILITH, according to late Kabalism.

" X.   LILITH [1] is, however, according to another tabulation,
the averse correspondence of *Malkuth*, with
whom later Kabalism connects NAHEMA, [2] the
demon of impurity." [3]

THE SATANIC HIERARCHIES

Lofty Intelligences, *Dhyan Chohans*, the Archangels and
angels of Kabbalism, direct both the involutionary and the
evolutionary processes and ensure their " success ".   Those
assisting on the downward arc tend to be regarded by man
as Satanic.   Those active on the upward arc are regarded as
redemptive.   Scriptural allegories present them as antagonists
and man looks upon them as devilish and divine respectively.
In reality, they are mutually equipoised powers working for
temporarily opposite objectives.

The Irish poet, James Stephens, intuited and expressed
this profoundly occult teaching in his poem, *The Fullness
of Time:* [4]

" On a rusty iron throne,
Past the furthest star of space,
I saw Satan sit alone,
Old and haggard was his face;
For his work was done, and he
Rested in eternity.

---

[1] According to the Zohar she is a stryge who slays infants.
[2] A succubus who brings forth spirits and demons after connection with man, says
the Zohar, which in various places further developes this idea.
[3] *Op. cit.*, pp. 79-81.
[4] *Collected Poems*, James Stephens, McMillan & Co., Ltd., London, 1931.

" And to him from out the sun
Came his father and his friend,
Saying,—Now the work is done
Enmity is at an end—
And He guided Satan to
Paradises that He knew.

" Gabriel, without a frown;
Uriel, without a spear;
Raphael, came singing down,
Welcoming their ancient peer;
And they seated him beside
One who had been crucified."

THE NATURE OF EVIL

Pneumatology apart, Satan as the personification and incarnation of pure evil has, in occult philosophy, no existence by himself. Evil is but the absence of good. It exists only for him or her who is made its victim. *Demon Deus inversus est.* The Devil is the shadow of himself which a man sees when he turns his back to the light. Nature is neither good nor evil, and manifestation follows only unchanging and impersonal law.

The existence and human experience of the duality of spirit and matter, light and darkness, motion and inertia, expansion and contraction, cause man to think of these as good and evil respectively. If resistance provides a fulcrum, then it is regarded as good. If it frustrates—as by the all-too-familiar " malice of the object "—or harms man, then it is evil in his eyes. The analogy of the searchlight partly illustrates this. Outside the beam and, as it were, pressing upon it from every side, is darkness. Light and darkness are perceived as a pair of opposites. The light-giving effects of the beam ceases at the limit of its range. There darkness begins. Thereafter darkness reigns. The instant the current is switched off, darkness reigns everywhere. If light is good, then the searchlight might be classed by man as good and the darkness as evil. But what, in fact, is that darkness which man calls evil? It is matter not subjected to light.   Darkness is unlighted matter.   Man calls it evil, and for him the Devil personifies this state.

Plotinus, in his Tractate on *The Nature and Source of Evil*,[1] translated by Stephen McKenna and B. S. Page, says:

> " Evil is from the Ancient Kind which we read is the underlying Matter not yet brought to order by the Ideal Form.
>
> " Given that The Good is not the only existent thing, it is inevitable that by the outgoing from it or, if the phrase be preferred, the continuous down-going, or away-going from it, there should be produced a Last something after which nothing more can be produced; this will be evil.
>
> " As necessarily as there is Something after the First, so necessarily there is a Last; this Last is Matter, the thing that has no residue of good in it; here is the necessity of evil."

To this, whilst concurring, the occultist would doubtless add " according to the mind and values of man ".   For in their essential existence, spirit and matter are neither moral nor unmoral, neither good nor bad.   They exist as apparent opposites; that is all.   Matter appears to resist spirit.   But so does the fulcrum of lever, yet without a fulcrum, leverage is impossible.   So, apart from human values and human experience, evil as an actual creation does not exist.   The origin of evil is in the mind of man.   All things can appear as either evil or good, according to human experience and human use of them.   Shakespeare echoed this teaching in his words: "Nothing is either good or bad, but thinking made it so." [2]

---

[1] The Medici Society Ltd., London.
[2] *Hamlet.*

PART IV

CO-OPERATION

CHAPTER I

CEREMONIAL AS A MEANS OF CO-OPERATION BETWEEN ANGELS AND MEN

THE INDWELLING LIFE

THE ministry of the angels, a cardinal doctrine of many faiths, has long been a living reality to a great many people. Occult research supports the doctrine, revealing that, as part of that ministry, certain Orders of angels are regularly present at religious Services [1] and certain other Ceremonials; for whenever superphysical forces are evoked and directed, whether by means of thought and will alone or by the use of symbols, signs and words of power, appropriate Orders of angels at once appear as the natural agents of those forces. Their function is both to conserve and direct the forces generated by ceremonial action, prayer and adoration and to serve as channels for the power and the blessing which descend in response. This ministration is far more effectively carried out when recognised by ministrants and congregation.

Two other aspects of the subject are, however, worthy of consideration. There are the effect upon the evolving life in Nature of Church Services such as the Celebration of the Holy Eucharist and the participation in human worship of the nature spirits and the Angelic Hosts. A digression is,

[1] Vide *The Science of the Sacraments* and *The Hidden Side of Christian Festivals*, both by The Rt. Rev. C. W. Leadbeater, and *The Inner Side of Church Worship* by Geoffrey Hodson, T. P. H., Adyar.

however, necessary in order to present the point of view from which I write concerning the life and consciousness of Nature. Under certain conditions of heightened awareness,[1] the universal, indwelling, divine Life becomes visible, though translation of such vision into brain consciousness and words presents many difficulties. When this state is attained, the divine Life in Nature is seen as an all-pervading, glowing, golden Life-force, omnipresent as an ensouling principle in every atom of every world. Physical forms then disappear. One is within and part of an all-pervading ocean of golden, glowing Life, which consists of myriads of points of light, interconnected by lines of force, the whole being part of an apparently infinite, living web [2] of exceedingly fine mesh which pervades all beings, all things, all worlds. Each of the points is found to be a source of Life, almost a sun, within which Life-force wells up as from an inexhaustible fount. From these centres, the golden power flows along the great web, vitalising all substance. There is no dead matter. All beings and all things are seen to be filled with the indwelling Life or Fire of God.

An inspired poet [3] truly described this state of consciousness:

" Lo! Heaven and earth are burning, shining, filled
With that surpassing glory which Thou art.
Lost in its light each mortal weakness, stilled
Each rapt adoring heart."

In the light of this vision, it would seem that the life of Nature is quickened every time the Holy Eucharist and certain other rituals are performed. The degree of response varies in each of the kingdoms of Nature and depends upon evolutionary development. In the mineral kingdom in which consciousness " sleeps " it is relatively dull; in the plant in

---

[1] Induced by contemplation of a scene or object of great beauty, enjoyment of a work of art, participation in an act of worship or meditation upon a spiritual truth.
[2] Vide The Web of the Universe, E. L. Gardner, T. P. H., London.
[3] Rev. Scott Moncrieff. St. Alban Hymnal.

which consciousness " dreams " it is greater; in the animal and in nature spirits, in both of which consciousness " awakens ", it is greater still; and in self-conscious beings such as angels and men it is greatest of all. At each Celebration, the power of response throughout the five kingdoms is increased, and this aid in the attainment of heightened awareness is part of the usefulness of every valid religious Rite.

In illustration, Nature may be likened to a plant which depends upon sunlight for its growth and flowering. If, after many cloudy days, the sun suddenly appears in all its brilliance, the life-processes of the plant are greatly stimulated, as the experiments of Sir Jagadish Chandra Bose, the great Indian scientist, so clearly demonstrated. If, in addition, the sun itself could be brought down to the plant without harming it and the plant receive into itself directly and individually an added measure of sunlight, then its whole growth would be correspondingly stimulated. It has seemed to me that a similar but spiritual, quickening occurs at Holy Communion, when the Lord Christ, the Sun of Divine Love, as also the Son of God, in His own Person draws near to all Nature and through the Sacred Elements is received by man.

THE HOLY EUCHARIST

My understanding of this wider significance of Church worship was deepened by observation of the response of Nature and the participation of the angels at an open-air Celebration of the Holy Eucharist [1] in Java. The selected site of the temporary Church, which was a garden on the slopes of Arjoena Mountain, permitted a splendid view across a great plain to Mount Kawi and, in the remote distance, to Mount Semeroe.

[1] The Liturgy of the Liberal Catholic Church was used; St. Albans Press, 30 Gordon Street, London, W. C. 1. The description given is not to be regarded as an advocacy of Catholicism, but only as a record of attempted observation of some of the superphysical effects of the Celebration of the Holy Eucharist. The Theosophist studies comparative religion and finds a certain group of ideas to be common to all world faiths and the exclusive possession of none of them.

Before the service began, nature spirits assembled near the Church in large numbers, attracted by the preparations and the intent of all concerned. As might be expected in this lovely land of luxuriant tropical vegetation, fairies and tree-spirits predominated in this assembly, whilst the great mountain Gods participated from their stations above their respective peaks. In addition, certain high Gods of earth, water, air and fire attended, as would seem to be the case at every such Celebration, when they contribute their special power and direct the participation in the Service of their subordinates and the forces of their element. This is especially noticeable at the *Offertorium*, in which all Nature seems to unite with man in the offering of the elements and in self-surrender to the Lord of Life.

As angels and nature spirits from near and far thus shared in human worship, the Celebration in Java assumed a magnitude far beyond anything visible at the physical level. At the moment of Consecration when, as always, the Power and the Presence of the Lord descended in a golden radiance, with the Host at its heart, the angels bowed low in reverence. The Life in all Nature in the neighbourhood of the Church seemed to glow more brilliantly. The consciousness of mineral and plant seemed to awake and respond, as the glory of His Presence shone from the altar as the truly magical words of Consecration were uttered. Angels joined mentally with the human congregation in fullest measure in the *te adoremus* and *adeste fideles*, their participation appearing to be far more vivid than man's, since human consciousness is dulled by incarnation. At the *ite missa est*, as is usual, the spiritual forces generated by the whole ceremony were liberated upon the world, angels accompanying them on their spiritualising mission. The Gods of Nature and the nature spirits, having received into themselves these quickening forces, later released them into those aspects of Nature with which they were variously associated.

Thus, externally, through the Rite which He instituted, and by the co-operation of angels and men, the Lord of Love keeps His promise to be with us " always even unto the end of the World". Interiorly, He needs no ceremonial to keep this promise; for in His mystical at-one-ment with the Spiritual Selves of all mankind, He pours into them His perfected and quickening Life and Light and Power. Even so, awareness in consciousness of His perpetual atoning Ministry could be aided by united worship in forms found to be elevating to those of various temperaments.

CHAPTER II

ANGELIC CO-OPERATION IN
THE MAYAN, HINDU AND JEWISH RELIGIONS

THE DEVIC SEAL

WHILST ceremonial intelligently performed is one of the most effective means of co-operation between angels and men, it is by no means essential. The human mind is a powerful broadcasting and receiving station. When empowered by strong will, trained in concentration and illumined by intuitive recognition of the unity of life, the mind becomes an exceedingly potent instrument.

When human thought is strongly directed towards a particular Order of angels, a mental signal is despatched and received by members of that Order. If the sender has attained to a certain universality of consciousness, and his motive is in consequence entirely selfless, the angels will unfailingly respond. Man may then direct his thought-force into, and himself enter, the chosen field of work, assured of angelic co-operation.

This combined activity may consist of such ministrations to others as spiritual healing,[1] inspiration, protection, or aid in overcoming weakness of character. Collaboration may also be sought in order to achieve needed inspiration in the execution of altruistic work. Angels are powerful allies in

[1] Vide descriptive material accompanying Plates Nos. 24, 25, and 26.

such ministrations, being able both to open up the channels of inspiration between the higher consciousness and the brain and telepathically to convey a train of illuminating ideas to receptive minds.

The regular practice of invoking the help of the angels is found to produce a change in the human aura. The link thus formed is visible as an area of brilliant light vibrating at the frequencies characteristic of the auras of the angels. When this *devic* seal, as it is called, is vivified by ceremonial action or by thought and will alone, it " transmits " a signal. on the wave-lengths of the particular Order of angels whose aid is being invoked. This call is then " picked up " by the angels to whom it corresponds in terms of vibratory frequency. Their attention thus gained, they are at once ready to render assistance.

Although clairvoyance is of help in this process, it also is not essential. Regular practice, based upon intuitive recognition of the truth of these ideas, will quickly provide strong evidence, if not proof, of the reality and efficacy of co-operation between angels and men. Such co-operation is indeed, continually occurring in the realm of the Higher Self of man, unaware of the fact though the lower self may be.

As previously stated, each of the well-established nations of the world is presided over by an angel Ruler who assists the race in the fulfilment of its destiny. These great Arch-angels—" Thrones " in Christian angelology—inspire the nation through the national Ego or Oversoul, and its leaders through their Higher Selves. Under such conditions of angelic inspiration, a statesman becomes possessed of powers hitherto unsuspected in him. As long as he selflessly serves his nation, his power will grow. Should selfish interests blind him to his duty to the State, angelic and other inspiration would be withdrawn and his power decline, a phenomenon

not infrequently observable in the lives of public men. Whilst
such co-operation is always available and is not infrequently
given, its effectiveness is greatly increased when it is initiated
and recognised by man.

The Gods were thus recognised by the peoples of olden
days and their aid was invoked.   Belief in them by the peoples
of ancient Egypt, Greece, Assyria and India should not, however, be regarded as evidence of polytheism.   The existence
of one Supreme Being was always recognised, the Gods being
regarded as subordinate manifestations of aspects and powers
of that One Alone.   These beings were not mere figments of
the imagination, nor were they solely personifications of
natural forces, laws and phenomena.   Occult research reveals
that certain of them had a real existence and were none other
than the Angelic Hosts with whom the people of those days,
particularly the Initiates of the Sanctuaries, consciously
co-operated.

MAYAN GODS

Interesting records of such collaboration have been discovered in Central America. According to the researches
of Ricardo Mimenza Castillo of Yucatan, who has for many
years been interested in Mayan research, this ancient people
practised co-operation between angels and men.   Apparently
every department of life was supposed to be presided over by
an appropriate deity.   Here is a list of them as given in the
St. Louis Star [1]:

" Hunab-Ku, comparable to Zeus, goddess of medicine;
Ixazahualoh, goddess of weaving; Ixchebelyax, goddess of
painting; Zuhuykah, goddess of virginity; Zitholontum, god
of medicine; Xocvitun, god of singing; Akinzoc, god of
music; Pizlimtec, god of poetry; Kukulcan, god of war;

---

[1] I regret that the date of publication was missing from my original notes and that
later searches through the files have not revealed it.—G. H.

Ahchuykak, the twins of the past and of attributes; Acate, god of commerce; Mutulzec, god of tortures; Chas, god of agriculture; Tabai, god of fishing; Kinichkakmo, god of fire; Ztab, god of suicide; Ekxhuah, god of travellers; to which are to be added the following tutelary deities: Kinch Ahan Haban, god of Campeche; Chun Caan, god of T-ho; Kabul, god of a place not known, but also the right hand of Izamal; Kakupacat, god of fire and Hun Ahau, also known as Yum Kimil, god of the underworld.

" To make these names pronounceable, it should be stated that Mayan and Aztec " x " had the sound of " sh " in English.

" Whether by accident or relationship, many of these Mayan gods had their counterparts in the mythology of the Greeks. For instance, the Mayan underworld was very similar to that presided over by Pluto. It was a place wrapped in eternal darkness and all those cast into it for transgressions in life suffered without end from cold, hunger, thirst, sleepiness, tortures, the sight of cruel spectacles, and were obliged to keep on wandering in the fashion of the Wandering Jew.

" The Mayans also had their heaven or paradise. It was an abode blessed with an ideal climate in which all plant and animal life flourished as nowhere in this physical world. The souls that were translated into this Elysium spent their time in what may be called the Platonian discussions of the purpose of existence and the true nature of the supreme God. From these labours they rested by listening to music and regaling themselves with perfumes and other delights.

" This heaven was presided over by four Bacabes, the Bacabe being a sort of angel, one of whom sat at each of the principal cardinal points and was assisted by one of the Chaques, gods of wind and rain. The four Chaques were of different hues. The one in the north was white, the one in the south yellow, he in the east, red and he in the west, black.

" The underworld was under the rule of Abcatanas, whose duty it was to foster the sacred tree with its four roots and four branches. Here, as in the celestial regions, everything was arranged in fours, due possibly to the notion of the Mayans that the earth was a square plane.

" In Chicen-Itza, Hunab-Ku, the Supreme, is pictured as the god from whose eyes flow two streams of tears, one to the right and one to the left of him. From these streams rise all floral and faunal life. The general interpretation of this is that Hunab-Ku is engaged in the creation either as act of sacrifice or grief.

" All in all, the Mayan concept of religion was unusually spiritual and refined and lacked entirely the grossness of what came to be known as the religion of the Aztecs, a similar people living contemporaneously on the Tableland of Anahuac, more especially the tribes that inhabited then the valley of Mexico.

" The Mayan temples resemble the structure of the Aztecs in their major feature which was the pyramid base of the sanctuary. It is still a question whether the Mayan borrowed this important detail from the builders of the pyramids who left the ruins at San Juan Teotihuacan, in the valley of Mexico, to tell their heroic tale; or whether the Mayan remains at Chicen-Itza were the prototype."

The sound of these unusual names is very interesting. Experimenting with them, I found that they have a distinct *mantric* [1] value. A continuous repetition of some of them, with a strong intent to evoke its possessor, has the effect of calling certain of these Mayan Gods and Goddesses. Here is an interesting field of experiment for any reader who is sufficiently sensitive to know when an answer is obtained to

---

[1] A *mantram* is a scientifically chosen word or sentence of power, by the utterance of which magical results and expansions of consciousness can be produced.

an evocation of this kind, *which, however, should never be made without a definite and lawful purpose.*

The Mayan angels present a characteristic appearance, their faces somewhat resembling those of Mayan and Peruvian statues. Many of them seem to have close affinity with the sun and with sun worship. Kakupacat, for example, would appear to be a salamander of great power and to be associated with solar fire resident in the centre of the earth, also that manifested through volcanoes. Kinichkakmo apparently re-presents surface fire and the element of fire generally. A point of interest in the account of the Mayan Gods is the reference to the four Bacabes of the cardinal points with their assistant Chaques and symbolic colours. Of these, the God of the East was red, that of the North, white, that of the South, yellow and that of the West, black.

THE DEVARAJAS

Hinduism is replete with information concerning the Gods and prescribed methods for their invocation. The Hindu name of the *Devaraja*, or Regent, of the East is Dhritarashtra, Lord of Air, and for His subordinate hosts, *Gandharvas*, their symbolic colour being white. This suggests the attribute of power for the East, as in the Mayan arrange-ment, which in its later epoch was possibly contemporary with early Indian civilisation. The *Gandharvas* are the *devas* of music, embodiments of the power of the sound of the creative " Word ". The Hindu name of the *Devaraja* of the West is Virupaksha, Lord of Fire, and His hosts, Nagas, their symbolic colour being red. The Hindu name for the *Devaraja*, or Regent, of the South, is Virudhaka, Lord of Waters, and His hosts are called Kumbhandas, the symbolic colour being blue. The *Devaraja*, or Regent of the North, is called Vaish-ravana, also Kuvera, Lord of Earth, and His hosts are the Yakshas, the symbolic colour being golden.

ACCORDING TO THE HEBREWS

Some Jewish traditions say that there are four Orders
or Companies of angels, each with an Archangel Head, the
first Order being that of Michael, the second of Gabriel, the
third of Uriel and the fourth of Raphael. The Cherubim
were angels of the power of the strength of God. They seem
to have been associated with the East or, as it was called in
the Temple, the Mercy Seat. St. Paul, describing the ancient
rites of the Jews in his *Epistle to the Hebrews*, Chapter IX, says:

" And after the second veil, the tabernacle which is called the Holiest
of all; . . . and over it the cherubims of glory shadowing the mercy seat."

The Archangel Michael, who is the Angelic Head of the
Ray of power, would seem to be the Ruler of the Cherubim,
for in *Genesis* III, verse 24, we are informed:

" He placed at the east of the garden of Eden Cherubim and a flaming
sword which turned every way to keep the way of the tree of life."

The esoteric teachings of the Hebrews known as the
Kabbalah are replete with information concerning the Angelic
Hosts. Reference is made to them in Part III.

THE WHEEL TURNS

Evidence of the reality of the Orders of the angels and
of co-operation with them is thus afforded by the similarity
of the descriptions which are to be found in the separate
records of the various ancient races and peoples of the world.
Since those days, humanity has entered a cycle in which intellectual development, in its early stage destructive of intuition
and mystical experience, predominates and from which only
now it is beginning to emerge. When in the present cycle
the phase is entered corresponding to that in which communion
occurred between Gods and men in preceding cycles, the
angels will again be seen by men and their functions made
the subject of scientific research. Such a phase I believe to

be now approaching.   Indeed, signs of it are not wanting in the world to-day.

In twenty-five years of world travel, I have found that the angels are living realities to an increasing number of people. Many students of occult philosophy regularly invoke their aid in healing, in Temple, Church and Masonic ceremonials and in meditation for the purpose of radiating spiritual power, blessing and peace upon the world.   As man's ethical and social wisdom develops he will be entrusted with deeper knowledge of Nature's hidden forces, laws and processes. In the new age of brotherhood and peace the dawn of which, despite many signs to the contrary, may even now be seen, there are grounds for hope that angels will once more walk with men.

CHAPTER III

THE RADIATION OF POWER

THOUGHT-PROJECTION

I N this Chapter information is offered concerning the means whereby spiritual and mental forces may be evoked and, with angelic co-operation, radiated upon the world. Such knowledge may be used both for evil and for good. All selfish use of spiritual power is evil. Occult activity for material self-benefit, with the deliberately chosen motive of personal advantage, is black magic. Misery inevitably follows its practice. The employment of spiritual and mental powers for the welfare of all mankind, without thought of return, is white magic and brings blessings to the world. May those who read on be inspired to use impersonally, dispassionately and solely for the welfare of the race the knowledge conveyed in this Chapter.

The mind and brain of man are powerful mental radio stations. Thought moulds not only the character of the thinker, but also that of all recipients of mental broadcasting. The impress produced by the thought of man upon fellow man helps to form individual and national characteristics, and influences both human destiny and the progress of civilisation. So intimate and unceasing is this psychical interaction, that all share in the achievements of each, whilst at the same time few can wholly dissociate themselves from responsibility for the widespread ugliness, cruelty and crime which are the curse of this planet. For these last are the products of ugly, cruel and criminal thoughts.[1]

When people combine in groups, their power to influence mentally the thought, character and conduct of others is multiplied. The tremendous potentiality for good of groups of dedicated and trained servants of the race who combine to use their thought power for beneficent purposes at once becomes obvious; for service of incalculable value could be performed by such groups. In this work, unity of both purpose and method is of supreme importance. The existence and maintenance of perfect harmony between the members of such groups is essential; for discord would be accentuated by the play of the forces generated and evoked. There must also be wise direction and careful choice of both leaders and members of thought-projection groups.

The ideas to be projected must be selected with great care. Unquestionable and unchanging truths alone may be safely broadcast; for every truth has behind and within it its own spiritual force. Every philosophic verity is a power as well as an idea. Thought upon a truth taps the power of that truth. Thought-projection by mental affirmation and verbal expression of a truth liberates that power. Ideas selected for projection must therefore subscribe to at least three rules. They must be basically true, non-compulsive (being sent out as offerings only) and wholly beneficent in their influence. In addition, to produce the maximum effect, they must be conceived and affirmed impersonally and with complete clarity.

Members of thought-projection groups should therefore be spiritually minded people, moved solely by a sincere

1 Vide *Thought Forms*, Annie Besant and C.W. Leadbeater, and *Thought Power, Its Control and Culture*, Annie Besant, T. P. H., Adyar.

aspiration to serve. They must be capable of impersonal effort in which they have no leading part, being ready, once a trusted leader has been appointed, completely to subordinate the personality. They must also be capable of clear thought, sustained concentration and powerful mental affirmation. They should not be mediumistic, unduly negative and passive people being unsuitable for this kind of work. The seeing of visions during supposed meditation, response to presences, desire to describe them and a general concern with personal psychism, are inadvisable in members of groups organised solely for positive and impersonal activity. Members must also be able to meet regularly and consistently for group work, and to maintain silence; for such work loses power when indiscriminately discussed.

The co-operation of the Angelic Hosts can be of the greatest value in such activities. Again a warning must be given; for two dangers exist. One of these is that faith in and attempted co-operation with the angels might degenerate into mere superstition and self-deceit. Against this, the experimenter must ever be on guard, being above all things a realist with a severely practical mind. The other danger is that heightened mental power and glimpses of the co-operating Intelligences might produce the illusion of the receipt of personal favours, and so lead to the evil of pride. Perpetually preserved impersonality and humility are the safeguards against this second danger. Since the Angelic Hosts are the embodiment of impersonality, universality of mind is necessary for man to be *en rapport* with them. Only as man universalises his consciousness can he enter the Kingdom of the Gods.

Angels are associated with the Power, Light and Life aspects of Nature. When Power is evoked from the Universal Source, focused by man's mind into a stream and then impersonally and accurately directed into a chosen field the Angelic Hosts are provided with suitable conditions for their natural activities. One of these is to conserve, direct and employ as a " tool " the energy of cosmic electricity. This force can be tapped and released at spiritual, mental and psychical levels. The will and mind of man, conjoined as in thought projection, both impress this energy with a mental characteristic and direct it into chosen fields. As the power goes forth on its mission, it must be carefully conserved and accurately directed if it is to produce its greatest effect upon receptive minds.

If their co-operation can be obtained, the angels associate themselves intimately with this focused current of force, conserve it against loss in transit and rapid dissipation on arrival and apply it with maximum effectiveness. Clarity of thought and keenness of concentration in the human operators are, however, still essential to success.

SUN RITUALS

In addition to this purely mental method of co-operation, bodily posture, gesture and movement, and colour and words, used with concentrated will-thought in simple ceremonial may, for certain temperaments, facilitate the process of collaboration with the Angelic Hosts. Such Rituals may be employed to evoke beneficent forces and distribute them upon the world.

Some thirty people recently participated in this method in the open-air in New Zealand. The ladies wore flowing Grecian dresses with long sleeves, and sashes and head bands coloured according to the nature of the influence to be invoked and radiated. The men were dressed in white flannels and wore similarly coloured sashes. Orange, blue, green and rose were used in rituals invoking and radiating power, purity, healing and love respectively.

The participants marched out upon a large lawn and stood facing inwards in three concentric circles, with a flaming brazier in the centre. They then began each of the four Rituals by saying together, slowly and with full intent:

"I dedicate myself as a channel for spiritual power (purity, healing, love, in successive ceremonies) to the world. I salute the Angelic Hosts."

With arms raised above the head and eyes turned upwards:

"In reverence I invoke spiritual power (purity, healing, love) from our Lord the Sun. I invoke the co-operation of the Angelic Hosts."

Turning outwards and lowering arms to a horizontal position:

"May spiritual power (purity, healing, love) pour forth upon the world."

Walking outwards for four paces, the participants, with utmost concentration and in co-operation with the Angelic Hosts, mentally directed the invoked power upon the world. Arms were then lowered to sides, with the words:

"Peace, peace, peace."

Turning inwards, all raised and joined their hands at the throat, bowed their heads and said in unison:

"Homage and gratitude to the Source of Light. Greetings and gratitude to the Angelic Hosts."

Hands were then lowered and the Ritual was brought to a close. A leader gave the time for all the movements and choral speaking, both of which had been carefully practised.

These Rituals were based upon ideas suggested to me by the angel who inspired my book, *The Angelic Hosts*. Sun Rituals are therein described somewhat as follows:

For the worship of the Spiritual Sun no other temples are needed than the free and open places of the world, the sunlit mountain-tops and plains, the fair valleys, and the open fields, the woods, the meadows and the hills. Withdraw yourselves from every artificial form and draw near to Nature's heart. Assemble, as the angels do, in companies inspired with but a single aim—the worship of the sun. March in stately processions, practise Rituals, engage in joyful dances, chant splendid litanies expressive of the glories of Our Lord the Sun. Standing in circles, in imitation of His glorious form, raise your open hands to the sky. Pour forth your love, your worship and your praise, acknowledging Him as Lord of all your lives.

Invoke His presence, His power and His life into your midst. Build, by your united thought and aspiration, a chalice to receive the wine of His ever outpoured life. That precious wine shall fill the cup, shall flow into your hearts and lives, and charge you with the power and the splendour of the sun. Your souls shall be irradiated by His light, your wills become resistless with His power, and your hearts be filled to overflowing with His love.

Thus illumined and refreshed, turn your faces outwards, stretch forth your hands and, with concentrated will, pour out His power and His blessing upon the world. The circle shall become like a sun; for His glowing splendour shall descend among you and effulgent beams shall shine through you to bless, quicken and bring peace to all your world.

With united wills and overflowing hearts, mentally flood all your world with the power of the sun. Thereafter turn your thoughts upwards in gratitude and reverence to the Power's Source. Close the Ritual by walking slowly outwards from the centre, forming, as all move together, the symbol of His outpoured light and life and love.

Graceful flowing robes in the colours of His spectrum may be worn and the wearers so arranged that His glorious hues may best be displayed. Patterns may be formed with solid blocks of colour, long straight lances, interwoven and blended lines and circular arrangements of the different shades in imitation of His rays. Artists shall design the robes and Rituals. Musicians shall compose the music for the chants,

odes, hymns and litanies which poets shall write. So may
the worship of Our Lord the Sun be once more established
on your earth and His kingdom be made manifest among the
nations of the world.

                *   *   *   *

Collaboration between angels and men is also enjoined
by its angel inspirer in my book *The Brotherhood of Angels
and of Men*. There it is written:

" Angels and men, two branches of the family of God,
may be drawn into close communion and co-operation, the
chief purpose of which would be to uplift the human race.
To this end the angels on their side are ready to participate
as closely as possible in every department of human life and
in every human activity in which co-operation is practicable.
Those members of the human race who will throw open heart
and mind to their angelic brethren, will find an immediate
response and a gradually increasing conviction of its reality.

" While the angels make no conditions and impose no
restrictions upon the activities and developments resulting
from co-operation, they assume that no human brother would
invoke them for personal and material gain. They ask for
the acceptance of the motto of the Brotherhood (of angels
and of men)—The Highest [1]—and its practical application
to every aspect of human life. They ask those who would
invoke their presence to develop the qualities of *purity, simplicity, directness* and *impersonality*, and to acquire knowledge
of the Great Plan whereby the ordered march of evolutionary
progress is maintained. In this way every human activity
will be founded upon the teachings and doctrines of that
Divine and Ancient Wisdom which has always reigned supreme
in the councils of the Angelic Hosts."

---

[1] The title of the frontispiece and a Chapter in the above-mentioned work.

PART V

ILLUSTRATIONS

INTRODUCTION

THE fifth part of this book consists of Miss Quail's striking pictures and my remarks upon them. As she has painted them to my descriptions, she is responsible only for their execution, not for their composition, colouring or form.

Appropriate portrayal of the appearance of the Gods is, in fact, impossible through the medium of paint applied to a plane surface. Coloured light or fire moving in three dimensions would be needed to produce the effect of intense brilliance, translucence, delicacy and constant motion characteristic of the radiant forms and shining aura of the Gods. Despite especial care and repeated observation, exactitude of description of these beings is almost impossible to one of my limited clairvoyant faculty. The continual changes in the colours and their arrangement, in the direction of the flow of auric forces and in the varying patterns produced, make accuracy exceedingly difficult.

At least two differing conditions of the auras of the Gods are discernible, one of expansion and the other of contraction. In expansion, the attention is outward-turned upon the divine Life and Mind in Nature. The aura is then greatly extended outwards from the central form and frequently, also, from behind in three-dimensional, wing-shaped radiations. In this phase, the component forces are flowing at their full power, which produces a great brilliance throughout the whole aura and a dazzling brightness at the various force-centres or wheels. In contraction, the attention of the God is directed towards the source of all Life and Power. The aura then becomes relatively quiescent and, with the exception of the radiations above the head which may increase in both dimension and brilliance, is much reduced in size. Examples of both of these phases are included in the accompanying pictures, although most of them represent that of expansion. The texture or grain of the aura is exceedingly fine and, despite Miss Quail's splendid achievement, has so far proved impossible of perfect portrayal. There are various layers of force within this aura, each with its own hues and direction of flow. The general effect is of brilliantly coloured, three-dimensional, shot moire silk, composed of flowing forces rather than substance and in constant, wavelike motion. Through this in many cases, from within outwards, streams of radiant energy, often white and of dazzling brightness, are continually flashing.

The direction of the flow of these auric currents is generally upwards and outwards from force-centres in the middle of the head and at the brow, the throat and the region of the solar plexus. Outlining the central form there is also a fine radiation, usually white or golden in colour. The head is nearly always crowned by upward-flowing, flame-like forces, which bestow upon the more highly-evolved Gods an appearance of regal splendour. For the most part, the universal energies for which the Gods are agents and directors descend from above the head and flow through the aura, greatly increasing its electric quality and brilliance. Other energies appear to arise directly within the body and *chakras*, as if from higher dimensions. As stated earlier, one function of the Gods appears to be to transform, in the electrical sense, these forces by means of the resistance offered by their bodies and by passage through their force-centres. Two of the results produced by this procedure are the transmission of spiritualising force into the substance of the lower planes of Nature down to the physical and the passing on of great currents of " stepped down " energy for the use of the angels and nature spirits in their various tasks upon these planes. Matter itself thus gradually becomes increasingly charged with spirit and so more malleable and responsive to consciousness and the forms of Nature gradually resemble more nearly the archetypal ideal.

According to occult philosophy, the superphysical worlds, which are the abodes of the Gods, consist of matter of increasing tenuity of substance ranging from the density of the finest ether up to the rarest and most spiritualised condition. These are six in number and each has its own inhabitants, human and angelic. In terms of human awareness in them, these planes may be called the emotional, the mental, the intuitional and that of the spiritual will. Above these four, but at present beyond the range of normal human awareness, are two others which will be entered by later races of men more highly evolved than ourselves.

The planes of Nature, seven in number if the physical be included, and each consisting of seven sub-planes, interpenetrate each other, each more subtle plane also extending much further beyond the surface of the earth than those below it in terms of density. They are of two orders, called the form and the formless worlds. The form worlds, in one classification, consist of the physical, emotional and four lower sub-planes of the mental plane. They are so called because in them form predominates over force and rhythm. The bodies in these worlds tend to be concrete and objective, with relatively clear-cut edges, particularly at the physical and mental levels. The formless worlds, which consist of the three higher sub-planes of the mental plane and those of intuition and spiritual will, are so called because in them life and rhythm predominate and form is reduced to its essence or Archetype.

The illustrations represent Gods inhabiting both of these groups of worlds. In the formless, where auras predominate over bodies, they appear as glowing centres of power surrounded by outflowing energies of many hues, almost veiling the form within. In the form worlds, the suggestion of bodily shape is greater, though here also, the shining aura frequently conceals the lordly and the beautiful form. For this reason the outer auras have been omitted from many of the pictures. In all cases, it should be remembered, the Greater Gods are surrounded by far-flung auras of many brilliant hues.

PLATE 1

A SEA NATURE SPIRIT

As far as my experience goes, variations of this type of primitive sea fairy are commonly to be seen skimming the surface of the oceans and the lakes of the world. Relatively undeveloped, the sea nature spirit has as yet little or no form. There is a rudimentary head which is the seat of consciousness, whilst a current of streaming white force suggests a body ánd a wing. More complex examples, with two or even more wing forms, are also to be seen.

These creatures fly about the surface of the oceans in innumerable hosts. Sometimes they rise high into the air; at others they plunge into the water to reappear in a few moments in a flash of white light, catching the eye with its brilliance. After a moment's concentration required to focus the appropriate power of vision, the swiftly moving, bird-like form appears to the observer, somewhat as painted by Miss Quail. The distance from head to tip of wing would vary from three to twelve feet, according to phase of manifestation and stage of evolution.

PLATE 2

A SEA SYLPH

The sea nature spirit evolves into the type of sea sylph here portrayed. This example has reached individualisation and, with countless similar and different beings, may be seen in the upper air, chiefly above the seas. The average height of the central form at this level of evolution would be from ten to fifteen feet.

PLATE 3

A SALAMANDER

This picture represents a fire nature spirit as described on page 130.

PLATE **4**

A MOUNTAIN SYLPH

This is one of the many types of non-individualised sylphs commonly to be seen in the air over the land. It is in swift motion, with shining inner aura streaming in beautiful, wing-like shapes behind and above it.

Interpenetrating and extending beyond the form and aura here portrayed are the finer radiations, not shown on the Plate, characteristic of every member of the Angelic Hosts. They are generally ovoid, composed of many brilliant hues, and extend for several yards on every side of the beautiful form within.

The orange sylph is possibly associated with the solar life-force or *prana* [1] with which the air is charged, and which constitutes the vitality of all organic forms. The height of the central figure of the sylph is about five feet.

---

[1] vide *The Etheric Double*, A. E. Powell, T. P. H., London.

PLATE 5

A LORD OF THE TREE FERNS

Whilst the building Orders of the Gods play all important parts in solar and planetary creative processes, another Order is concerned with the evolution of consciousness within the form. This ministration to the evolving life in the mineral kingdom is considered in Part II, Chapter I. Trees and forests also receive similar assistance, the classical concept of the dryad of the trees being founded upon fact. Nearly all well-grown trees have attached to them, in addition to innumerable nature spirit builders, an advanced nature spirit or a God which throughout its life remains within or linked to the astro-etheric double and the aura of the tree. The presence of such a being, through the constant play of its thoughts and auric energies, greatly quickens the evolution of tree life and consciousness. Such nature spirits and Gods are subordinate to more advanced beings in charge of groups of trees of the same genus, as are found in large woods, forests and jungles.

As an aid to comprehension of the effect of the presence of nature spirits and Gods upon the consciousness in mineral and plant kingdoms, one may think of a bowl of still water as representing the sleeping group consciousness of hill or mountain, plant or tree. Goldfish placed in this bowl would by their movements keep the water in continual motion, and this is in part the effect produced upon mineral and plant consciousness by the presence and play of the thought and auric forces of nature spirits and Gods.

Quaint, animal-headed nature spirits were found embedded within the trunks of well-grown tree ferns in the jungles on some of the mountains of Malaya and Ceylon. They were quite primitive beings, with little or no external awareness. Indeed, they gave the impression of being fast asleep. The plant growth and reproductive processes would be felt by them as faint stimuli, for they are growing with the trees, being intimately associated with their cell life and consciousness.

The tree fern God here portrayed was observed over the jungle in the mountain district of Ceylon, near Newara Eliya. Such a being assists the evolution of form and the unfoldment of consciousness of a very large number of tree ferns. It is of interest to observe that the patterns formed by the flow of the lines of force in the aura of this God reproduce within it certain of the tree fern forms. An explanation of this is suggested in the description accompanying Plates 13 and 14.

The central form of this being is some fifty feet tall. The aura, however, is capable of extension for at least one hundred yards in all directions and was thus expanded when first seen high in the air, about a mile away. In the picture the outer aura is omitted and the inner aura is shown in phase of contraction, as when the God graciously hovered for a few minutes of mental communion. Through both form and aura currents of force, presumably from the tree fern Archetype, play down into successive areas of the jungle as the God moves above its domain and ministers to its charges.

PLATE 6

A LORD OF THE PINES

This being was observed in association with groups of stone pines in the Cape Peninsula, South Africa. As the picture shows, the colouring and the lines of force in the inner aura—the outer is omitted—suggest somewhat the needle-like foliage of the pine. Many well-grown pines were found to have their own tree God resembling the one here portrayed, but smaller in size and lower in evolution. The stature of this God is about thirty feet.

PLATE 7

A TREE NATURE SPIRIT

This sixteen-year-old Waringan tree grows in a garden in Madioen, in the Island of Java. It was planted by the lady of the house, who became much attached to it and felt it to be a living, conscious being from whom, she assured me, she received a sense of friendliness and rest.

When taking tea beneath its welcome shade, I became aware of the presence of this delightful tree nature spirit or dryad. I found it to be approaching individualisation, or evolution out of group into individualised consciousness,[1] and to be well aware of the affection of the owner of the tree and responsive to it, which would beneficially affect its development. This nature spirit is approximately five feet tall.

[1] For a full description of this process as it occurs in the animal kingdom, vide *The Causal Body*, A. E. Powell, T. P. H., London.

PLATE 8

A MOUNTAIN GOD

Here is portrayed a mountain God intimately associated with the element of fire. It was observed at Loskop Mountain, near Harrismith in the Orange Free State, South Africa. The remarkable arrangement of the auric forces and the brilliant colóuring are unique in my experience. Both are well portrayed in this fine example of Miss Quail's art. The central figure at the time of observation was partly within the mountain and some fifty feet tall. A greatly extended outer aura, here omitted, shone with similar but more delicate hues.

PLATE 9

A MOUNTAIN GOD

This being was observed in the Drakensberg Range in Natal. Two of the most striking features were the remarkable mitre-like effect produced by the uprush of forces from the head and shoulders and the brilliant, four-funnelled force-centres in the region of the solar plexus through which power was flowing into the mountain below. The axes of the rapidly spinning funnels formed an equal-armed cross, the arms of which met within the form of the God and pointed forwards, backwards, to the right and to the left. In this picture the effect of translucency, characteristic of the appearance of all the Gods, is well portrayed. In the process, however, the impression of the tremendous power of the God and of the passage through it at high voltage of mighty forces from above, also of brilliance and radiance, is perhaps, not conveyed quite so adequately as in other pictures.

Watching this God throughout successive days, I was reminded constantly of the vision of Ezekiel.[1] Certain currents in its aura were arranged in the shape of upward-pointing wings, far more three-dimensional than any picture could suggest. The *chakras* received and compressed the descending forces, which were then directed into the mountain below. The central form in this case is at least sixty feet tall and it is one of the most majestic and splendid members of this Order of the Angelic Hosts that I have ever been privileged to behold.

PLATE **10**

A MOUNTAIN GOD

This God was also observed in the Drakensberg Range
in Natal, presiding over the region known as the Amphi-
theatre at Mont aux Sources.   I have more than once received
evidence of similarity of type and appearance in the various
Gods of one mountain range. Comparison with Plate 9
reveals a similarity between the two Gods of the Drakensberg
Range.   In both of them the wing-like radiations and the
intensely brilliant, vortical force-centres or " wheels " were
noticeably common characteristics. The God is shown in
phase of expansion, the auric wings extending at least half a
mile from tip to tip, whilst the outflowing and descending
energies have a very much greater range. In this picture,
part of the outer aura is included. The central form is at
least sixty feet tall.

PLATE 11

A MOUNTAIN GOD

This picture portrays the presiding God of a mountain range, which was observed high above one of the peaks of the Hottentots Hollands Mountains in Cape Province, South Africa. As I observed and gave my description to the artist, the downflow of power was so great and so brilliant as almost to conceal the form and aura of the God. The chief colours shown were lavender, gold and white, the central form of the God and the aura immediately surrounding it shining in those hues with a dazzling radiance quite impossible to reproduce. The uprush of golden-coloured, fiery power above the head was particularly brilliant, bestowing upon the God the appearance of a majestic *Deva* King wearing a crown of flames. In all cases of *devic* direction of natural energies, however prodigious the outpouring of power may be, the God always gives the impression of complete mastery of the forces flowing through and all about it. The central figure is at least eighty feet tall.

PLATE **12**

A MOUNTAIN GOD

This God was observed at one of the mountain peaks of the Table Mountain Range in the Cape Peninsula, South Africa. Evidently it has close affinity with the element of fire. The picture shows the inner aura and form alone and in phase of contraction, during which it is drawing into itself universal fire-power. This it directs in a concentrated stream, as an awakening force, into the mineral life and consciousness indwelling in the mountain below.

The upward-flowing streams above the head were enlarged into a cup or bowl of flame, reaching high into the heavens. Fiery energy was playing down into this auric chalice, from which it passed through the form in great sheets, streams and flashes into the surrounding atmosphere and the mountain below.

In phase of expansion, the God presented the most magnificent appearance. The auric forces then resembled tongues of flame shooting out for hundreds of yards on every side, as if he stood in the midst of a mighty conflagration. The central figure is about sixty feet tall.

PLATE 13 AND 14

A MOUNTAIN GOD

This God was observed in the Cape Peninsula, near the eminence known as Castle Rock, high above the Kirstenbosch Botanical Gardens. Apparently the establishment of the Gardens in this area has offered it an opportunity of extending its operations beyond the mineral and bush consciousness and forms of the mountain into those of the many wild and cultivated flowering plants; for when, studying it for the purpose of these pictures, I noticed that its beautiful lavender and green aura was frequently extended in a great sweep of force to include the whole of the Gardens.

The creative energy then flowing through the aura of the God produced within it the geometrical mental forms upon which the shapes of the plants and flowers are founded. This specialisation and intensification, explained in Part I, Chapter III, augments the form-producing capacity of the universal, creative power and thought. Plant *devas* and nature spirits similarly receive these forces, further specialising them and increasing their power accurately to reproduce in etheric and physical matter the plant forms conceived of by the Major Mind.

The High Gods and their individualised subordinates perform this work deliberately and self-consciously as servants of the One Will. Nature spirits serve instinctively in response to impulses natural to them, strengthened on occasion by their *deva* superiors. The ultra-microscopic builders and the

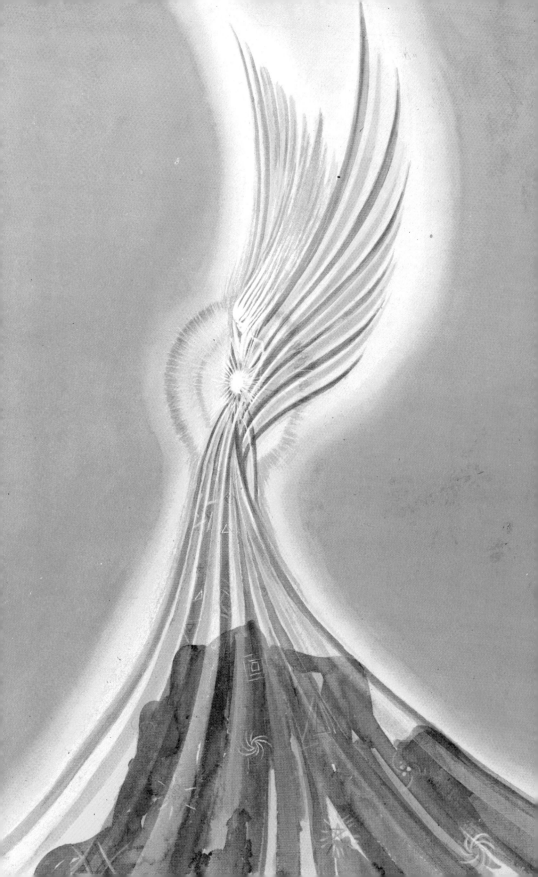

larger nature spirits perform their share in this creative process quite unconsciously. They play with and among the creative forces and the forms which they produce primarily in etheric matter. Their play is, however, quite purposeful, though they are unaware of the fact, for their movements cut lines of force in the ether which mark out the areas and centres of molecular, and later cell formation. All these processes and activities occur within the consciousness of the presiding God.

The second, profile picture shows in part the arrangement of the inner auric forces of the mountain God, the stature of which is about sixty feet. The outer aura is omitted.

PLATE 15

THE GOD OF A SNOWCLAD RANGE

In this picture an attempt is made to portray the second of the two Gods of the Sierra Nevadas in California, referred to in Part II, Chapter I.

In order to show the concentric arrangement, the colouring and the dazzling whiteness of the outer sphere, a cross section has been taken through the centre of the aura. The *devic* form is approximately fifty feet tall.

PLATE **16**

A LANDSCAPE GOD

This very great being is the presiding *deva* of an area of the Cape Province, South Africa, covering many thousands of square miles. It is stationed high above the region immediately to the north of the Karoo Desert, its sphere of influence extending to the coast where, at certain of the Capes, landscape *devas* are established. Natural forces from the South Pole and Antarctic continent flow northwards into South Africa, and doubtless other continents in the Southern Hemisphere. These Gods assist both the development of form and the awakening of consciousness in the mineral kingdom of the desert, plains and mountains of their region and at the same time conserve and direct the forces from the Pole.

Ambassadorial Gods were also perceived moving between the Antarctic and South Africa, whilst others maintained relations between the God here pictured and those of the mountains, jungles, deserts and plains to the North. On many occasions I have become aware of the operation of a system of *devic* inter-communication maintained by travelling Gods, who visit those stationed at important continental regions of the globe.

As indicated in Part II, Chapter II, I have received evidence of the existence of a great planetary, landscape God, so mighty as to be able to hold the whole Earth within its consciousness, a *Deva* King of the physical world. I have also observed the radiation from the centre and surface of the Earth out into interplanetary space of very powerful, natural energies. In addition, from the sun and the planets, and possibly from outer space, great forces reach the globe, as if the Earth were being subjected to a perpetual inflow of power. Moving amidst these interchanged forces, planetary and extra-planetary, Gods of power, like *devic* engineers, are to be seen. As in the case of the landscape God here portrayed, they appear to be responsible for the reception, specialisation and re-direction of these energies. This God is at least one hundred feet tall, whilst its auric forces are capable of extension to a distance of a great many miles.

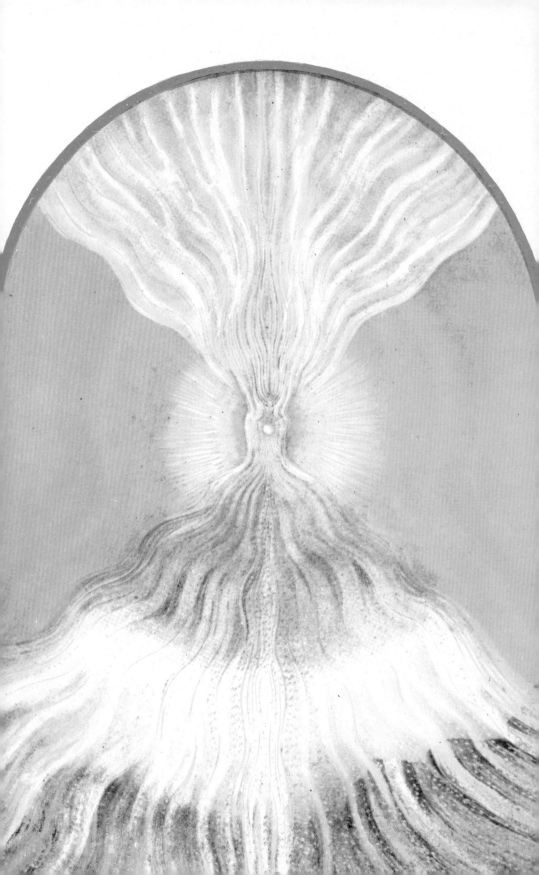

PLATE **17**

A GOD OF THE GOLD REEF

An exposition of creative processes, in which gold is used as an example, and the Gods of Gold are described, is to be found in Part I, Chapter III. This picture, whilst an accurate reproduction of my description, somewhat too much suggests human femininity. The descending gold-creative energies, the brilliant gold points or centres of force in the aura and the smooth, rhythmic flow characteristic of the force aspect of gold are, nevertheless, well portrayed. The lateral extension of the auras of these Gods was less than usual. The vertical extension, on the other hand, was immense, reaching from some two hundred feet in the air to at least the same distance below the surface of the veldt, whilst the actual gold-producing force played on down to the reef, in some cases six thousand or more feet below.

The central figure was unusually small for such an auric extension, being in this case little more than eight or ten feet tall. The presiding God of the Gold Reef is, however, colossal in stature.

PLATE **18**

A GOD OF THE SOUTHERN PACIFIC

This magnificent ocean God was observed from the south coast of Java. Apparently it is the ruling *deva* of the great area of the Pacific Ocean which extends from Java to Australia. At the higher mental level it is relatively formless, as here portrayed, though the unusual, pointed, oval shape produced by the flowing streams of its auric forces was clearly discernible. As the picture shows, great currents of power descend upon this sea God, are compressed within its aura and then released into the ocean beneath.

These forces are both creative and energising. All atomic and molecular patterns, and the forms of marine vegetation and of fish and their shells, are in part a product of these descending, creative energies. The sea God also directs powerful currents of quickening energy into the consciousness incarnate in every atom of the sea water and in the forms of the mineral, the marine plant and the fish kingdoms.

This being is subordinate to a still greater God, responsible for the whole Pacific Ocean, in its turn a Vice-regent of the planetary sea God, which performs similar functions (and doubtless many others as yet unknown to me) for the life and consciousness of the oceans of the world. The God here presented is similarly assisted by great hosts of subordinates in a descending scale of evolutionary stature, the more advanced of whom resemble it in appearance.

At the lower mental and emotional levels these Gods assume concrete shape and operate in oppositely polarised pairs. Thus, although there is no sex in the Kingdom of the Gods, the appearance of male or female or *deva* and *devi* is sometimes suggested according to preponderant polarity. Beneath these in evolution are the non-individualised sea nature spirits, and below them again the primitive beings portrayed in Plate 1.

Under the seas, different types of Gods and nature spirits are to be observed. On occasion I have seen huge, whale-like, etheric monsters drifting about somewhat aimlessly in the great depths. The Kingdom of the Sea is indeed a densely populated empire. It is presided over—chiefly, it would seem, from above the surface—by a very great being, the planetary God of the Sea.

PLATE 19

A GOD OF THE SOUTHERN PACIFIC

Occasionally the *deva* portrayed in Plate 18 descends to the " form " worlds, assuming there a definite shape somewhat as shown. Thus seen, it resembles some splendid Sea God from classical mythology, riding the waves upon a shell-like car.

The flowing curves of the aura resemble those of a shell and doubtless are partly produced by the passage through the God of creative energies expressive of the divine thought or Archetype of the shell form. In the higher worlds the God is of immense stature. In the lower, the central form is some thirty feet tall.

PLATE **20**

AN ANGEL OF MUSIC

True music is a temporary, physical expression of the sound of the ever-uttered " Word ". Throughout creative Day, the Great Breath is breathed upon the Great Deep, which responds as an aeolian harp of myriad, vibrant strings. As creative Night draws near, the Great Breath is breathed in. Thereafter silence reigns within the Great Deep.

The Monads of living beings are as breaths in the Great Breath. When at the dawn of creative Day the Voice first speaks, the innumerable lesser breaths contribute the component notes of the creative chord, which is the " Word ". When at creative Eve the Voice is stilled, the lesser voices die away. Thereafter silence broods upon the face of the Deep.

Thus behind and within material universes creative sound subsists, that celestial symphony of which Nature's forms are a physical expression. The " Word " itself exists in two phases, the pre-Cosmic and the Cosmic, the silent and the uttered. When " spoken ", the " Word " creates and releases the divinest harmonies and upon these, as dynamic Archetypes, the universe is built.

When the one creative Voice begins to speak, the ten divine Intelligences, the Archangels of the Sephiroth, the first manifested Lords of Light, hear and perfectly express the " Word ". This, as creative sound, they transmit throughout the new-born universe. Thereafter, the myriad

231

Hosts of the Logos receive and re-express the music of the " Word " in worlds of growing density.

Thus the Kingdom of Music is established, the citizens of which are the Spiritual Selves of angels and of men. In this Kingdom vast hosts of Archangels and angels re-echo the harmonies of the creative " Word ", thereby aiding in the construction of the first, archetypal, sound-built forms. Each of these beings is perpetually resonant with the component chords and notes of the basic theme of the universe, its idea-motif.

The loftiest Archangels first embody and re-sound the glorious harmonies of the " Word ", which are then relayed by their immediate successors in the hierarchical Order. Thence this wondrous music descends through successive ranks of shining beings, until the lower worlds of form are reached. There, too, the Angel Lords of mental and emotional realms re-echo the creative " Word ". Lesser angels and their younger brethren, the nature spirits, answer to the song, and by them the densest, material world is built according to the " Word ".

An Angel of Music, or *Gandharva* as it is known in Hinduism, is here depicted not as a portrait but as a type of celestial musician, the inner form only being shown.

A ROSE ANGEL

The six pictures which follow portray angels who are associated with aspects of divine consciousness, rather than with currents of creative Life-force and the mineral and plant kingdoms of Nature. Rose angels, such as the one here portrayed, may be thought of as incarnations of divine wisdom and love, qualities which bring them into intimate contact with the Immortal Selves or Egos of men. Association with such beings is indeed a privilege and their co-operation in the service of humanity can be of the greatest value.

The second picture is an attempt at portraiture. This closer view shows the various force centres. Those in the head are seen to radiate from a common centre, upward through the crown and forward through the eyes. As stated in the opening paragraphs of this fifth part of the book, no static medium, however skilfully used, can possibly convey the delicacy, the glowing radiance, the translucence, which contribute to the general effect of the intense brilliance and the supernal beauty characteristic of the Angelic Hosts. This is especially true of the ethereal, radiant, angelic incarnation of divine love portrayed in these two Plates. The large and glowing aura, chiefly rose, crimson and gold in colour, has been deliberately omitted from both pictures in order that the graceful central form, normally somewhat veiled within it, may clearly be seen.

When, in the performance of certain Rituals of Free-masonry and those described in Part IV, Chapter III, the power and influence of divine love are invoked and poured forth with angelic aid upon the world, angels of this Order would be likely to respond to the invocation and co-operate in the distribution of the power and its application to general and individual needs. This particular rose angel is some twelve feet tall.

THREE HEALING ANGELS

These pictures portray three different types of angels engaged in their healing ministry The general method is first to direct streams of purifying energy into and through the aura of the sufferer, in order to disperse congestions in the etheric and emotional bodies especially and to drive out harmful substances. They then re-attune the chord or " Word " of the individual, usually dissonant in the *psyche* during ill-health, and try to restore the harmonious and rhythmic flow of the inner Life-forces throughout the mental, emotional and physical nature. Finally, they invoke divine healing power which flows through their auras, as well as directly from its Source, into the patients, affecting them locally or generally, or both, according to the needs of the case.

Such ministrations are far more effective when man consciously invokes and co-operates with the healing angels. A successful method of spiritual healing with angelic co-operation consists of dwelling in concentrated thought upon the Lord Christ [1], the great Healer of the World. reverently entering His presence in thought and seeking to touch the " hem of His garment ", which means the fringe of His consciousness. The sufferer is then drawn mentally into His

[1] Followers of other Religions will here substitute the name used in their Faiths for the Source of healing life and power, whether universal or individual, solar or planetary. Buddhists and Hindus may decide, for example, to invoke the aid of " The Lord of Loving Kindness ", known in both Faiths as the Lord Maitreya, the Supreme Teacher of Angels and of Men the *Bodhisattva*.

Presence, being visualised as radiantly healthy and flooded throughout his whole nature with the golden, glowing, healing Life of God, as portrayed in these pictures. The following or similar prayer may then be uttered with powerful intent and a pause between each sentence:

" May the healing power of the Lord Christ descend upon (Christian and surnames of the selected suppliants). May the healing angels encompass them.'

After a pause of some minutes, during which the thought is powerful yet reverently centred upon the Lord Christ, His outpoured healing power and the healing angels, the meditation may be closed with the words:

" May the light of His love enfold them for ever. Amen."

Healing angels have been found to be continuing their ministering function for at least twenty-four hours after such an invocation. Regular practice by this or similar methods will quickly demonstrate the efficacy of angelic co-operation in spiritual healing. Those who participate are warned against the exercise of personal will in order to attain desired results. Once the healing power has been invoked, always with the fullest faith, the results should be left to the *karma* and evolutionary needs of the individuals. When there is a strong desire that some loved one should be healed, surrender to the divine Will and the great Law should be expressed in such words as " according to the Will of God " or " as may be most expedient for them ".

The occultist learns to work without thought of results. As said in Part IV, Chapter III, in no circumstances should he use his will power and occult knowledge to obtain by force, personal, material benefits for himself or for others. Such would be grey, if not black magic, the error into which Judas fell in selling his Lord for thirty pieces of silver. As Judas died by his own hand, so all who fall into this same error are in danger of a form of spiritual suicide.

PLATE **26**

AN ANGEL OF JAVA

A remarkable Buddhist Shrine, known as the Borobudor, was built in the Island of Java, some eight hundred years ago. This is an immense stone structure, with scenes from the life of the Lord Buddha beautifully carved on the sides of the four great galleries. This Shrine has become a place of pilgrimage and is regarded by many as a centre of spiritual power. Investigation revealed the presence of a very great presiding Angel, conserver and distributor of the power of the Shrine and source of potent spiritual forces which flow over the Island of Java and the surrounding seas.

The height of the central figure is probably from twelve to fifteen feet, but in the case of an Ego which attained Adeptship as man and then transferred to the Angelic Kingdom, the height of the body is not an indication of spiritual stature.

PLATE 27

A KUNDALINI DEVI

According to one view, *kundalini*—also called the Serpent Fire—is the power of giving or transmitting Life. *Prana*—known physically as vitality—is the power of organising Life. *Fohat*—known physically as electricity—is the power of using and manipulating Life. These three cosmic forces of the Third, Second and First Aspects of the Logos respectively are present as ensouling energies of all substances on every plane of Nature. *Fohat* is the universal constructive Force of Cosmic Electricity and the ultimate hidden power in this universe, the power which charges a universe with Life, with Spirit; it is described as the Will and the Mind, the very Self, of God. This supreme force is in all creatures. When specialised and enclosed within the spinal cord of man it is called *kundalini* or the power that moves in a serpentine path; hence its other name the Serpent Fire. In man, it is sheathed with care, but man must learn to set it free; for it is the God in him, without which he would cease to be.

Kundalini is in essence creative and, though as yet but slightly aroused, with all other forces and powers of Nature, is represented in the physical body of man. There, at this period of human evolution, it manifests itself as the source of both the sex impulse and the nerve fluid. It resides, coiled serpentlike, in the sacral *chakra* or " wheel " at the base of the spine, which in its turn is a relay station for the similarly coiled up energy in the centre of the Earth, itself a storehouse of solar *kundalini*.

When fully aroused, either by yoga or as a natural result of evolutionary progress, *kundalini* flows up an etheric canal in the spinal cord called the *sushumna nadi*, passing through each of the other *chakras* on its journey. As it passes through the spinal centres in which the *chakras* arise, some of its force flows down the axis of the funnel of each, vivifying it occultly and thereby awakening the individual to self-conscious awareness in the superphysical worlds.

When *kundalini* touches the spleen centre, it gives the power of travelling at will on the astral plane whilst away from the physical body. When it touches and opens the heart centre, the forces of the Buddhic or Christ consciousness in man resident in the vehicle of intuition,[1] if sufficiently unfolded, begin to flow through the neophyte at the physical level and the " mystic rose "—the heart *chakra*—" blooms " upon his breast. The powers of the Christ consciousness— knowledge of the oneness of life, direct, intuitive spiritual perception, wisdom and a profound compassion—then begin to manifest themselves through thought and word and deed. The throat centre, when vivified, bestows the power of clairaudience, or of responding to superphysical sound vibrations as well as to those physical sounds which are beyond the normal auditory range. The brow centre, when occultly vitalised, bestows the faculty of clairvoyance and when the coronal *chakra* is opened, the neophyte acquires the faculties of using superphysical awareness whilst still awake in the physical body and of leaving and returning to the body at will without any break in consciousness.

As *kundalini* rises up the *sushumna nadi* it is accompanied by two complementary forces, one positive and the other negative. Each of these flows along its own canal in the spinal cord, sometimes called *pingala* and *ida* respectively,

---

[1] Vide *Man and His Bodies* and *The Soul and Its Vestures*, A. Besant, and *Man, Visible and Invisible*, C. W. Leadbeater, T. P. H., Adyar.

though these names are also given to the forces themselves. These two oppositely polarised, *akashic* [1] forces meet and cross at each of the *chakras* as they rise, and finally pass, one of which in consequence becomes hypersensitive. [2] They then function somewhat as do the valves or the amplifiers of a radio receiving set, thereby enabling consciousness within the brain to pick up superphysical forces and become aware of superphysical phenomena. Indeed, the cerebro-spinal system of man, when occultly vivified, resembles in many respects a television receiving set. One difference, however, is that superphysical broadcasts are projected upon the screen of the mind-brain, and are clairvoyantly perceived. The full manifestation of these occult faculties during waking consciousness demands a long and ardous training, and depends upon the complete vivification of the pituitary and pineal glands by means of *kundalini* and its complementary forces.

In the paths followed by these three currents one recognises the caduceus, the staff of the God Hermes, consisting of a rod around which two serpents are coiled, a winged sphere crowning the symbol. *Kundalini* ascending the *sushumna nadi* is represented by the rod, and the forces flowing along *ida* and *pingala* by the two serpents, whilst the winged sphere symbolises in part the freed soul of the man who has awakened and learned to use these hidden powers. Such a man does indeed become as a Hermes, a messenger from heaven to earth; for he ranges free in the higher worlds and brings to men the knowledge and wisdom of those realms. Ultimately he also rescues or liberates Persephone, symbolic of the human soul, from the Underworld or normal limitations imposed upon it during waking hours by the occultly unvivified physical body.

---

[1] *Akasha*, Sanskrit, the subtle, supersensuous spiritual essence which pervades all space; a fifth element or principle in Nature, as yet undiscovered by physical science; the aether of the ancients; the substratum and cause of sound. Vide *The Theosophical Glossary*, H. P. Blavatsky, *Akasa, Azoth, Kundalini.*
[2] Vide *The Chakras*, C. W. Leadbeater, T. P. H., Adyar, and *The Science of Seership*, Geoffrey Hodson, Rider & Co.

Like all basic forces in Nature, *kundalini* is the manifestation of an Intelligence, an Archangel in fact, though of a nature beyond human comprehension. The picture in part portrays a glimpse unexpectedly obtained whilst passing through the preparatory stages which precede meditation. First a living caduceus was seen of intense, fiery power connecting earth and sun. Contemplating this, I seemed to become aware of a Solar Intelligence or *Kundalini Devi*, somewhat as here portrayed.

THE MIRACLE OF BIRTH
AND THE WORLD MOTHER

During investigations of pre-natal life [1] I constantly became aware of the presence and ministration of certain types of angels which were assisting in the dual process of the construction of the new bodies, mental, emotional, etheric and physical, and the induction into them of the reincarnating Ego. Though I did not realise it at the time, I have now come to believe that, during the involutionary arc or descent into incarnation of each life cycle, these angels perform for every individual a function closely resembling that carried out on behalf of the race by the *Pitris*, the so-called ancestors of man, sometimes occultly referred to as the Satanic Hierarchies.[2]

A study of these angels revealed them as agents of a great Intelligence which presides over and directs all maternal processes throughout Nature. The teachings of occult philosophy relate this Being to the Feminine or Mother Aspect of the Deity, of which She is a manifestation and a representative.

Matter itself, universal substance or *prakriti*, is the *arche* or womb wherein all worlds gestate, from which all are born and to which all return. The true World Mother is this primary substance of a universe when first differentiated from the root of matter or *mulaprakriti;* for therein reside the seeds

---

[1] Partially recorded in my book *The Miracle of Birth*, T. P. H., London.
[2] *Vide* Part III, Chapter, V, " The Inverse Sephiras and the Problem of Evil ".

of all living things and the powers of conservation and reproduction.

When differentiation occurs at the dawn of Cosmos, following the night of Chaos, the three Aspects of the primordial Trinity, the Creator, the Preserver and the Transformer, become self-manifest and creatively active. They are then represented by lofty divine Intelligences, Powers or Emanations, themselves the highest fruits of preceding *Manvantaras*, whose bodies are " of the essence of the higher divine light ". Intelligences of such a nature, when emanated from root substance, direct the course of evolution under immutable Law. They are no Beings such as the human mind can conceive. They constitute both the highest Sephirothal Triad and the Seven which proceed from Them, or rather the Spirit behind each. They may perhaps be described as Very Soul of the Very Soul of the universe.

The cosmic maternal Principle is universally manifest and its conserving and reproducing attributes are active throughout all Nature. Physically, it is expressed both as chemical, negative polarity and as femininity throughout the whole organic world. It is active within every single cell as also in every multi-cellular organism. Without it nothing could be conceived and born, nothing preserved, nothing reproduced. Superphysically, the maternal Principle is of equal importance. For man, it is the Auric Envelope, the *arche* of the Spiritual Soul, the *Augoeides* or Causal Body, the womb wherein gestate Initiate, Adept, Logos-to-be.

All nations have recognised, honoured and worshipped this maternal Principle in Nature. All their exoteric religions have personified it as a Goddess, an Archangel Mother of universes, races, nations and men. These personifications of the World Mother are amongst the very noblest concepts of the human mind, which in creating, reverencing and serving them reaches its highest degree of idealism, devotion and religious self-expression. Such reverence, such devotion and such worship as are offered to World Mothers are therefore worthy of the deepest respect and, gross superstition apart— ever to be resisted—may usefully be encouraged. For through human devotion, human beings may be reached from on high. Through human aspiration, highest love and suppli- cation, man is susceptible to both his own Spiritual Self and the influence of the Adept Ministrants of mankind. The Madonna ideal, for example, has been and still is of incalcu- lable value in consoling, purifying and ennobling humanity. Through it, a realisation of the Mother-Love of God has been brought within reach of millions of suffering and aspiring people. The concepts of Kwan Yin, Isis, Ishtar, Parvati and other Goddesses are similarly founded upon the existence, nature and function of the same great Being. Perhaps because I am a Christian and the cases I was examining were also Christian, the Madonna-like forms here pictured presented themselves to my mind.

The planetary World Mother is conceived in certain schools of occult philosophy as a highly-evolved Archangel Representative and Embodiment on earth of the Feminine Aspect of the Deity. She is also thought of as an Adept Official in the Inner Government of the World, in whom all the highest qualities of womanhood and motherhood shine forth in their fullest perfection.[1]

Since She is beyond all limitation of form, no picture can truly represent Her. In Plate 28 She, in a Madonna-like form, and Her ministering angels appear in close association with a mother and her unborn child as the time of birth draws near. Plate 29 symbolically portrays Her in Her solar aspect, brooding in divine love over all worlds.

In reverent salutation to Her as Queen of the Angels, I bring to a close this illustrated study of the Angelic Hosts.

[1] *Vide The World Mother as Symbol and Fact*, C. W. Leadbeater, T. P. H., Adyar.

A RETURN VISIT TO BOROBUDOR (IN 1971)

My previous visits to this great Buddhist Shrine in Java have been described as having revealed to me the presence of a very great presiding Angel, conserver and distributor of the power of the Shrine and source of potent spiritual forces which flow over the Island of Java and the surrounding seas. The height of the central figure is probably from twelve to fifteen feet, but in the case of an Ego which attained Adeptship as man and then transferred to the Angelic Kingdom, the height of the body is not an indication of spiritual stature.[1]

The kindness and generosity of friends in Sourabaya made possible a further visit in January, 1971. Although not thinking especially of this great Being at the time, whilst some seven or more miles still separated our party from the Shrine itself, I again became aware of the presiding presence and power of the *Devaraja*.[2] In consequence, I realised that its influence is by no means limited to the immediate region of the Shrine, but in varying degrees reached over the whole of Java and the seas and Islands far beyond. In addition, great rays of spiritual power shone forth in many directions throughout the superphysical worlds, as was partly indicated by the picture in my book.

[1] *The Kingdom of the Gods*, p. 237.
[2] *Devaraja*, Angel King.

Having arrived with our small party at the summit of the Shrine, I sought by meditation again and more deeply, if it might be, to receive such instruction as the Great *Devaraja* might deign to give... From his mind to mine there gradually began to flow a stream of ideas concerning the life, the force and the consciousness of the universe and their self-expression as angels and as men. This description of the process is not strictly accurate, however; because during such communication, the sense of duality is reduced to a minimum. Rather did the two centres of consciousness, those of the great angel and myself, become almost co-existent, temporarily forming one " being " *within* which the stream of ideas arose. This, I believe, is essentially true of all interchanges which occur above the level of the formal mind, and especially at those of spiritual Wisdom and spiritual Will. In the latter, it is assumed, duality virtually disappears and oneness, uttermost interior unity, alone remains.

The *Devarajas* and *Devas* whose consciousnesses and being are established in the *Arupa* worlds, are of themselves entirely free of any restrictions of location, even the idea of which can have little or no place in the higher *Manasic, Buddhic* and *Atmic* planes. When, therefore, one refers to an *Arupa Deva* by the name of a physical plane locality or centre, the title can be either incorrect or misleading, especially if it suggests spatial limitations which restrict the consciousness established at levels where the idea or space-location cannot exist.

How, then, it may be asked, may one permissibly associate an *Arupa Deva* with a place or even consecrated Shrine on the physical plane? A brief dissertation on the subject of Cosmogenesis may perhaps aid one's understanding or at least partially answer the question. All Creative Logoi, meaning Emanators of universes, may be thought of as voluntarily making a sacrifice which, in its fullness, is beyond the comprehension of man.

Timelessness, meaning absolute freedom from time-restrictions, and spacelessness, meaning absolute freedom from space-restrictions or even the remotest concepts of either of these—may be thought of as partially surrendered by both Creative Logoi and the Heads of those Hierarchies of Creative Intelligences who participate with the Logoi in the procedures of the objective space-time manifestation of THAT which is eternal and infinite.

One example of this surrender is an *Arupa Deva* who, in accordance with the procedures of involution and evolution and the Directors thereof, agrees to use specially selected places on Earth as centres through which the powers for which he is agent may reach the world of forms and so also the Life which is evolving within the restrictions of form. The very great *Devaraja* of Borobudor may, I suggest, be regarded as one who long ago became associated with the great Shrine for such purposes. The *Devaraja* is in no sense limited to that particular part or place upon the surface of the planet Earth, but voluntarily agrees to whatever limitation there may be in order to fulfil the functions which are assigned to it or which it has accepted.

These are in part to subjugate matter itself, particularly physical matter, to the rhythmic impact and interpenetration of forces which the *Devaraja* has " stepped down " from higher levels. Throughout the ages, this passage of energy through dense substance gradually reduces its inertia and so reduces the resistance of matter to Spirit, to evolving life and to spiritualising consciousness.

A second function, I gathered, is to reduce the degree of impenetrability or resistance to Spirit of the layers or highest sub-planes of matter of each of the planes of nature. As the ages pass, these barriers gradually become more readily penetrated by consciousness, this being one of the effects of the energy or " driving force " which the *Deva* directs into the substance of the *rupa* planes.

A third function consists of the subjection of the indwelling and evolving Life to the receipt and passage through it of energies which " awaken " it to gradually increased interior and external sensitivity and responses, thereby quickening the evolutionary processes. This third function is more especially helpful to the Life evolving through the organic kingdoms than the inorganic, although all Nature is stimulated and its evolution hastened by the Angelic Hosts. Thus, the " *Devaraja* of Borobudor " may be thought of as of planetary or terrene evolutionary stature and in no sense limited in consciousness to the great Shrine.

Such in part are thoughts which arose in my mind as I meditated on the summit of Borobudor.

L'ENVOI

" The Gods await the conscious re-union of the mind of man with the Universal Mind. Humanity awakens slowly. Matter-blinded through centuries, few men as yet perceive the mind within the substance, the life within the form.

" In search of power and wealth, men have traversed the whole earth, have penetrated the wilds, scaled the peaks and conquered the polar wastes. Let them now seek within the form, scale the heights of their own consciousness, penetrate its depth, in search of that inner Power and Life by which alone they may become strong in will and spiritually enriched.

" He who thus throws open his life and mind to the Universal Life and Mind indwelling in all things will enter into union therewith and to him the Gods will appear."

A Mountain God

BIBLIOGRAPHY

ABC of Atoms, The, (Bertrand Russell).
Angelic Hosts, The, (Geoffrey Hodson).
An Outline of Theosophy, (C. W. Leadbeater).
A Study in Consciousness, (A. Besant).

Bhagavad Gita, The, (Trans. A. Besant).
Brotherhood of Angels and of Men, The, (Geoffrey Hodson),

Causal Body, The, (A. E. Powell).
Chakras, The, (C. W. Leadbeater).
Clef des Mystères, (Eliphas Levi).
Collected Poems, (James Stephens).
Coming of the Angels, The, (Geoffrey Hodson).
Coming of the Fairies, The, (Sir Arthur Conan Doyle).

Devachanic Plane, The, (C. W. Leadbeater).
Doctrine and Literature of the Kabalah, The, (A. E. Waite).

Essential Unity of All Religions, The, (Bhagavan Das).
Etheric Double, The, (A. E. Powell).

Fairies, (E. L. Gardner).
Fairies at Work and at Play, (Geoffrey Hodson).
First Principles of Theosophy, (C. Jinarajadasa).

Gods of Egypt, The, (Budge).
Great Design, The, (Sir James Arthur Thompson).

Hidden Side of Christian Festivals, The, (C. W. Leadbeater).

Initiation and the Perfecting of Man, (A. Besant).
Inner Government of the World, The, (A. Besant).
Inner Side of Church Worship, The, (Geoffrey Hodson).

Journal of Parapsychology.

Kabbalah Unveiled, The, (S. L. MacGregor Mathers).
Key to Theosophy, The, (H. P. Blavatsky).

Lotus Fire, The, (G. S. Arundale).

Main Currents in Modern Thought, (Editor: F. Kunz).
Man and His Bodies, (A. Besant).
Man, Visible and Invisible, (C. W. Leadbeater).
Masters and the Path, The, (C. W. Leadbeater).
Miracle of Birth, The, (Geoffrey Hodson).
Monad, The, (C. W. Leadbeater).
Mysterious Universe, The, (Sir James Jeans).

Nature and Source of Evil, (Plotinus. Trans. S. McKenna).

Physics and Philosophy, (Sir James Jeans).

Reach of the Mind, The, (J. B. Rhine).
Reincarnation, Fact or Fallacy? (Geoffrey Hodson).
Review, The, (of Calcutta).

St. Alban Hymnal.
Science of Seership, The, (Geoffrey Hodson).
Science of the Sacraments, The, (C. W. Leadbeater).
Secret Doctrine, The, (H. P. Blavatsky).
Seven Human Temperaments, The, (Geoffrey Hodson).
Seven Rays, The, (Ernest Wood).
Solar System, The, (A. E. Powell).
Soul and Its Vestures, The, (A. Besant).

Theosophical Glossary, The, (H. P. Blavatsky).
Thought Forms, (A. Besant and C. W. Leadbeater).
Thought Power: its Control and Culture, (A. Besant).
Transcendental Magic, (Eliphas Levi).

Web of the Universe, The, (E. L. Gardner).
World Mother as Symbol and Fact, The (C. W. Leadbeater).

INDEX

INDEX

Symbols used: " n " means foot-note of page indicated
"*passim*" means item noted more than once on
or between pages indicated

A

A BCATANAS: Mayan Ruler of the under-
world, 192
Absolute (The): term for THAT, 3; Will-
Light is from, 25; Absolute Life, Absoluteness, 138; One Alone is first emanation from, 152; three veils of, 158; mentioned, ix, x
Achievement, Goal of, *see* Goal
Adam (of Genesis): Bible teaches angels in
existence before death of, 56; same as
Adam Kadmon, 159; Chokmah is
second, 160
Adam Belial: arch-demon of Chaigidiel, 175
Adam Kadmon: same as Adam (of
Genesis), 159
Adepts: as Supermen, 9; experience conscious unity with Creator, 9; have evolved
into cosmic consciousness, 12; perceive
directly the phenomenon of Nature, 21,
75 *passim*; Adept officials assist in choos-
ing type of life for reincarnating Egos,
77; bring Eternal Life and Eternal Substance into equipoise, 169; attain Nirvana, 171; adeptship, 237; World Mother
is Adept Official, 244; mentioned, 119,
171, 243
Adramelek: arch-demon of Samael, 176
Affection: nature spirits show for growing
plants, 36; shown by angels in colour
conversation, 91; angel uses to assist
human beings, 93; shown between angels,
96; tree spirit aware of affection of
owner, 216; *see also* Love
Agents of Karma, 73, 160, 165
Ahamkara: I-making impulse, 171
Ain Soph Aur: Ain is first veil of The
Absolute, 158, 160; Ain Soph is second,
158, 160; Ain Soph Aur is third veil, 158
Air: fairies and sylphs associated with element of, 56; third of the four elements,
103; Dhritarashtra is Hindu God of, 193

Aishim: term for cherubim, 164
Akashic forces: 240, 240n
Alchemy, 103
All (The): goal is to be fully conscious
of, xiv
All-Mother, 25
Almighty One: name for Metatron, 159
Ama: term for Binah, 161
Amazons: faces of sylphs resemble, 127
Ambassadorial Gods, 225
Amen-Ra, 140
Amoeba, 102
Ancient mysteries, *see* Mysteries
Ancient of Days: term for Kether, 159
Ancient Wisdom, 202
Angelic hierarchy: earth's angelic hier-
archies, 65-86; nature spirits among
lowest of its ranks, 98; serves as trans-
former for Logos, 133; of Kether, 160;
of Hod, 164; mentioned, 73, 83, 232
Angelic Hosts, The, by Geoffrey Hodson,
quoted, 130-133, 200-202
Angelic Hosts: defined, x-xi; teacher in-
structs author regarding, xviii; portrayed as husbandman, 8; assist in process of regeneration, 34; known also as
Sephirothal Hosts, 53; conception of in
occult research, 54-55; Angelic Hosts of
a Solar System manifested in one Solar
archangel, 67; nature spirits are among
lowest orders of, 68; in Fiery Cross, 70;
humans under care of, 77; Angel of
Religion transmits responses from, 78;
orders of assist World religions, 78;
maternal mind protects its progeny
through orders of, 82; emerge from
archangels, 138; ten orders of associated
with ten sephiras, 156; members of function at birth of human being, 173; participate in Holy Eucharist, 185; many
nations acknowledge existence of, 190;
Kabbala replete with information concerning, 194; afford co-operation in

251

P